Random

J. Mummey

ISBN-13: 978-1539987581
ISBN-10: 1539987582

DEDICATION

To my computer and the C# language: thank you for not spiraling into an unrecoverable crashing abyss moments before my publishing deadline.

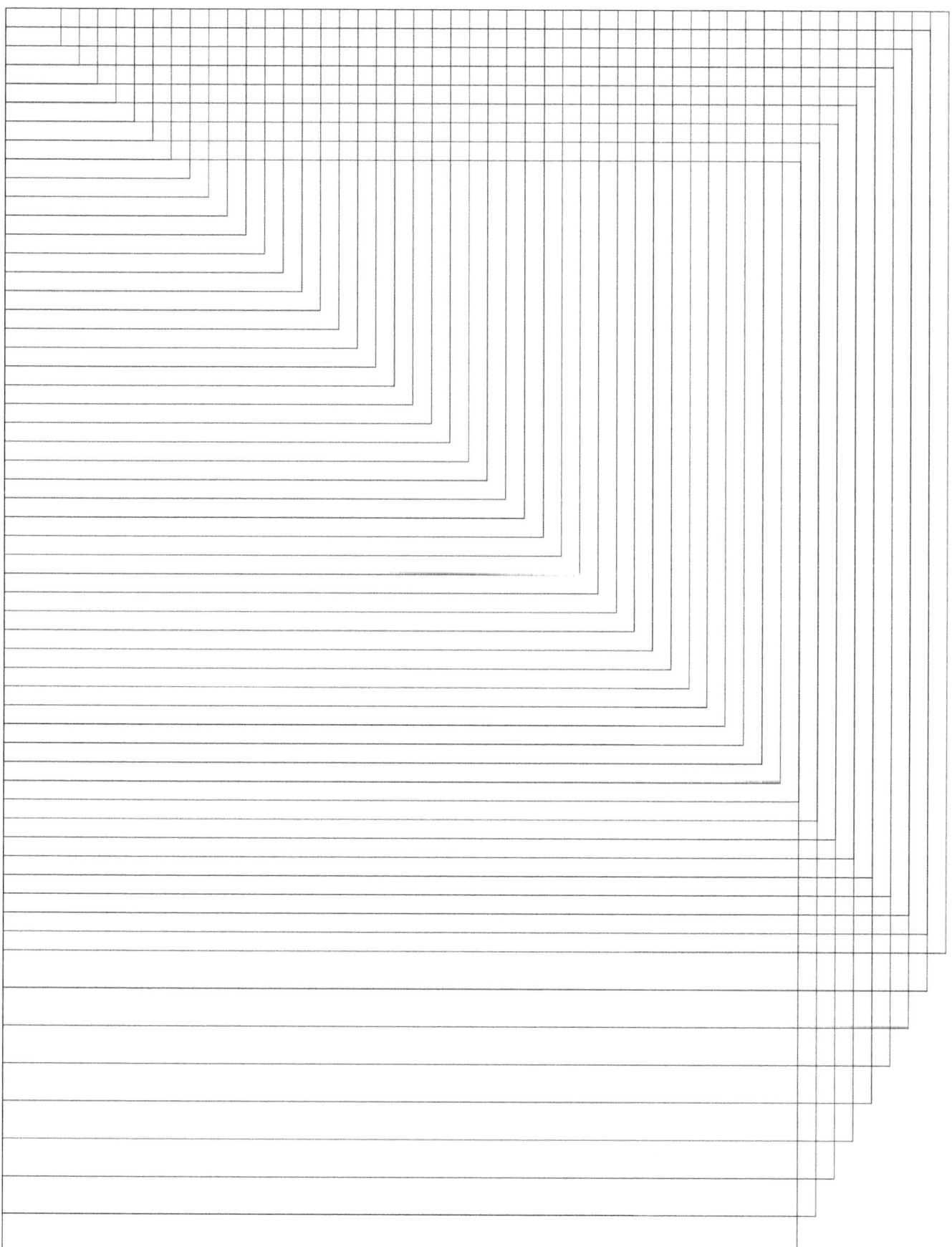

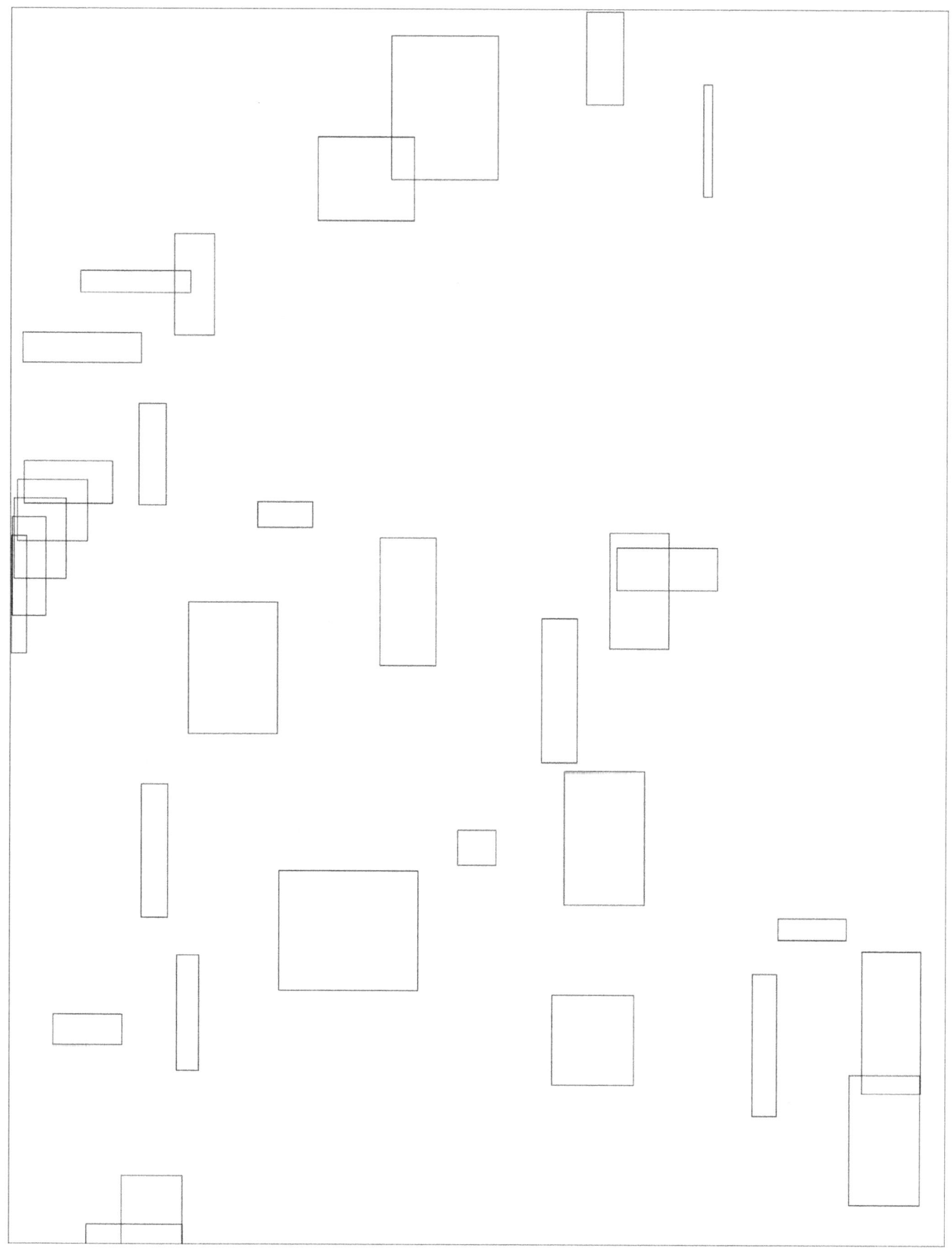

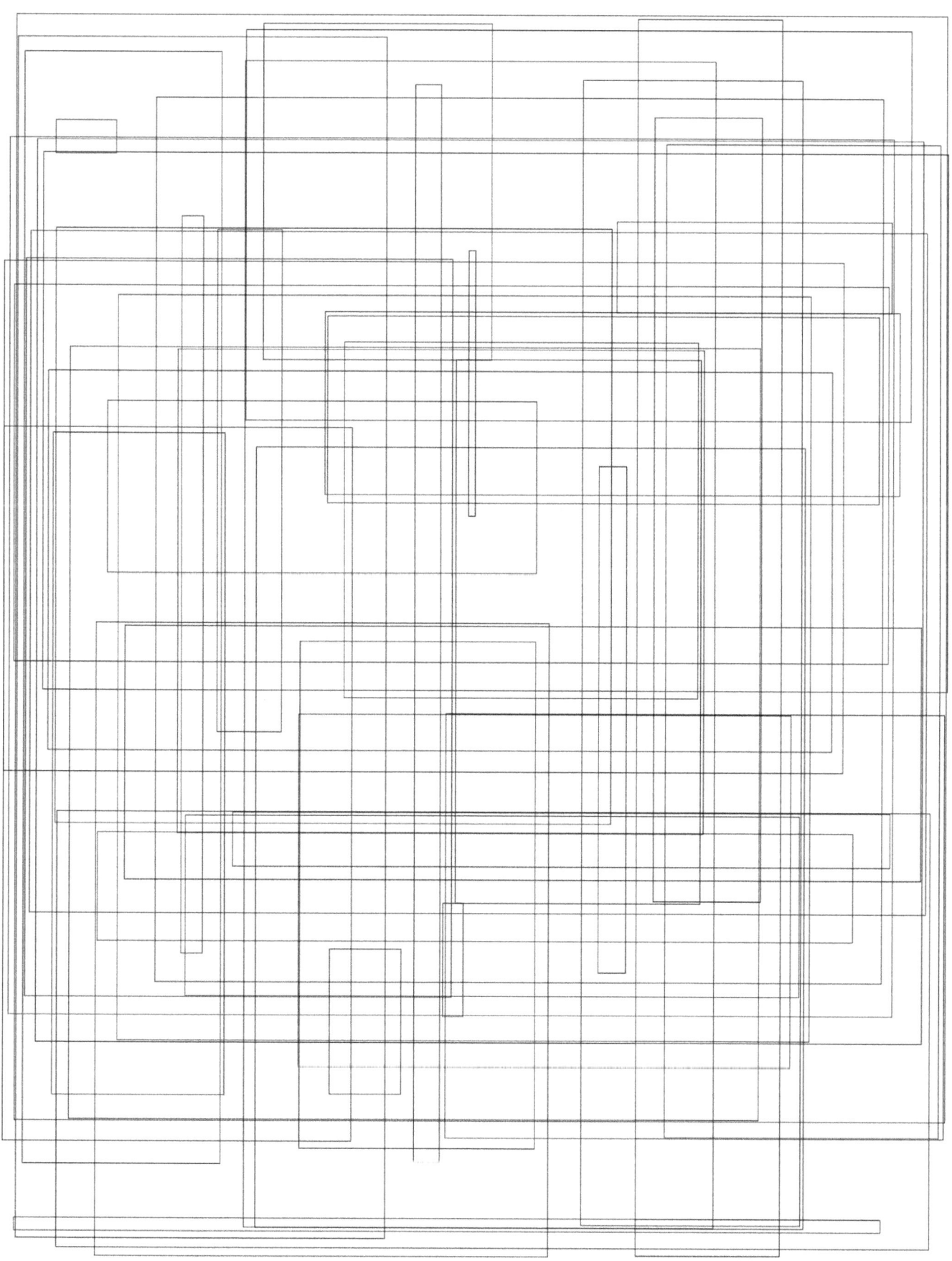

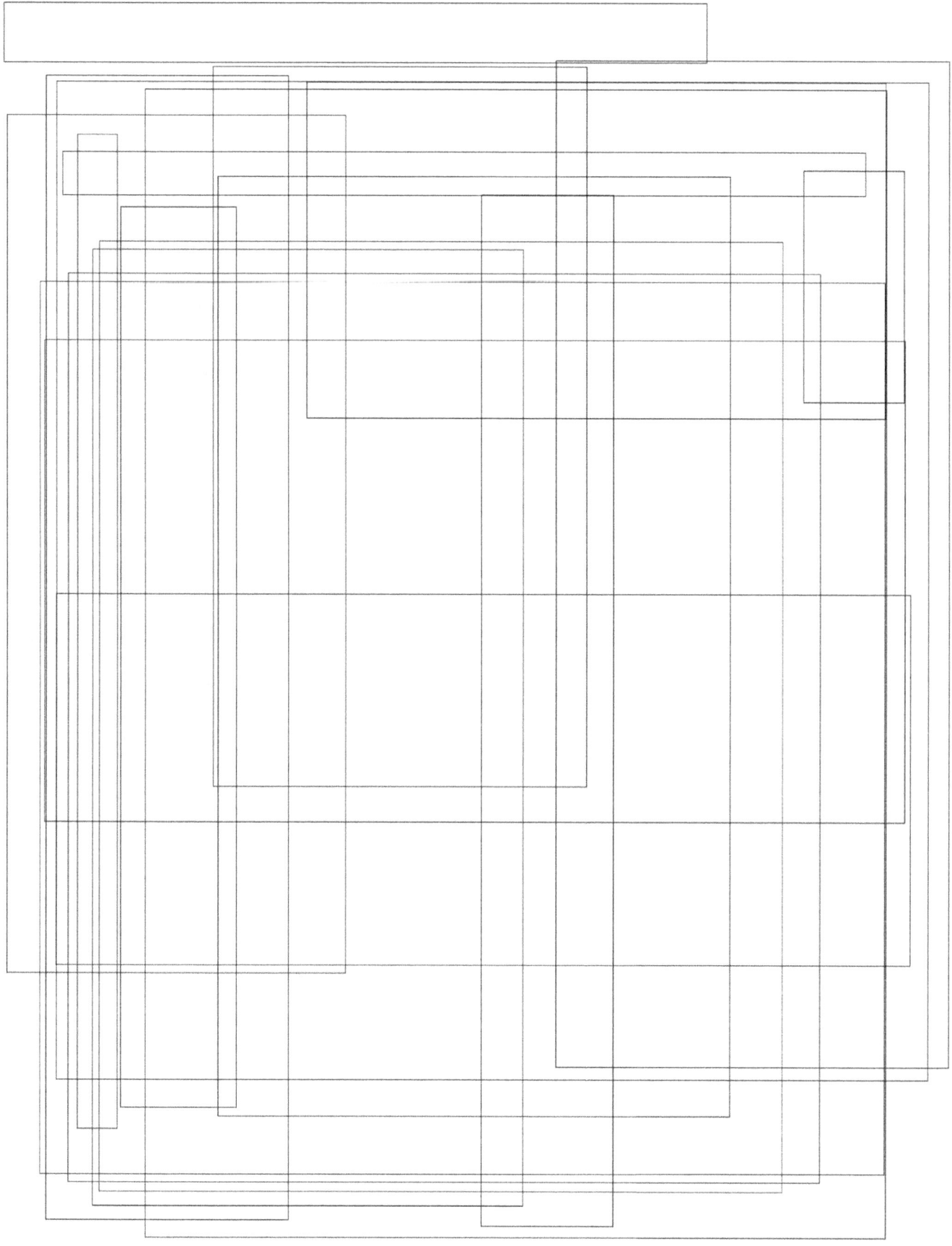

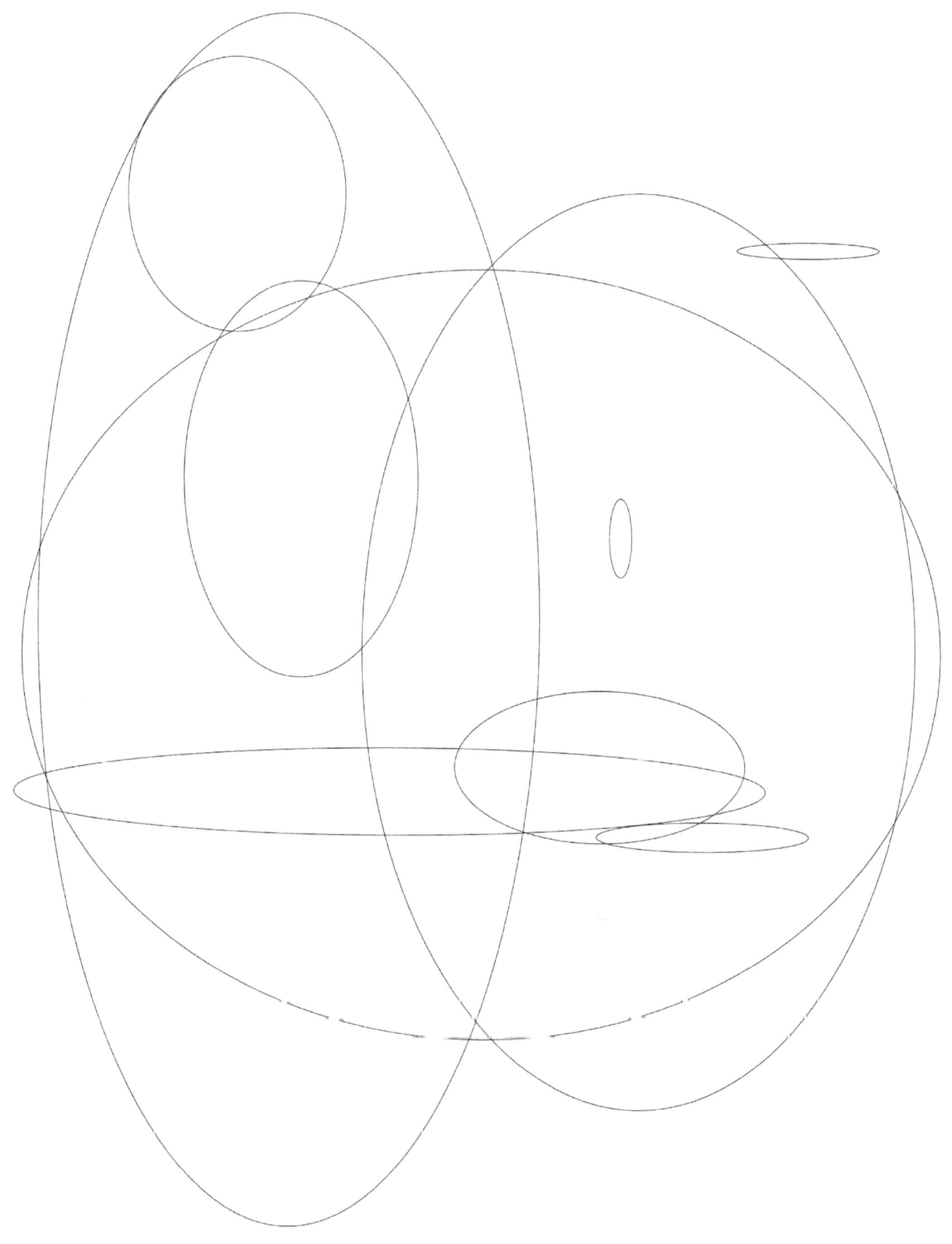

J. Mummey

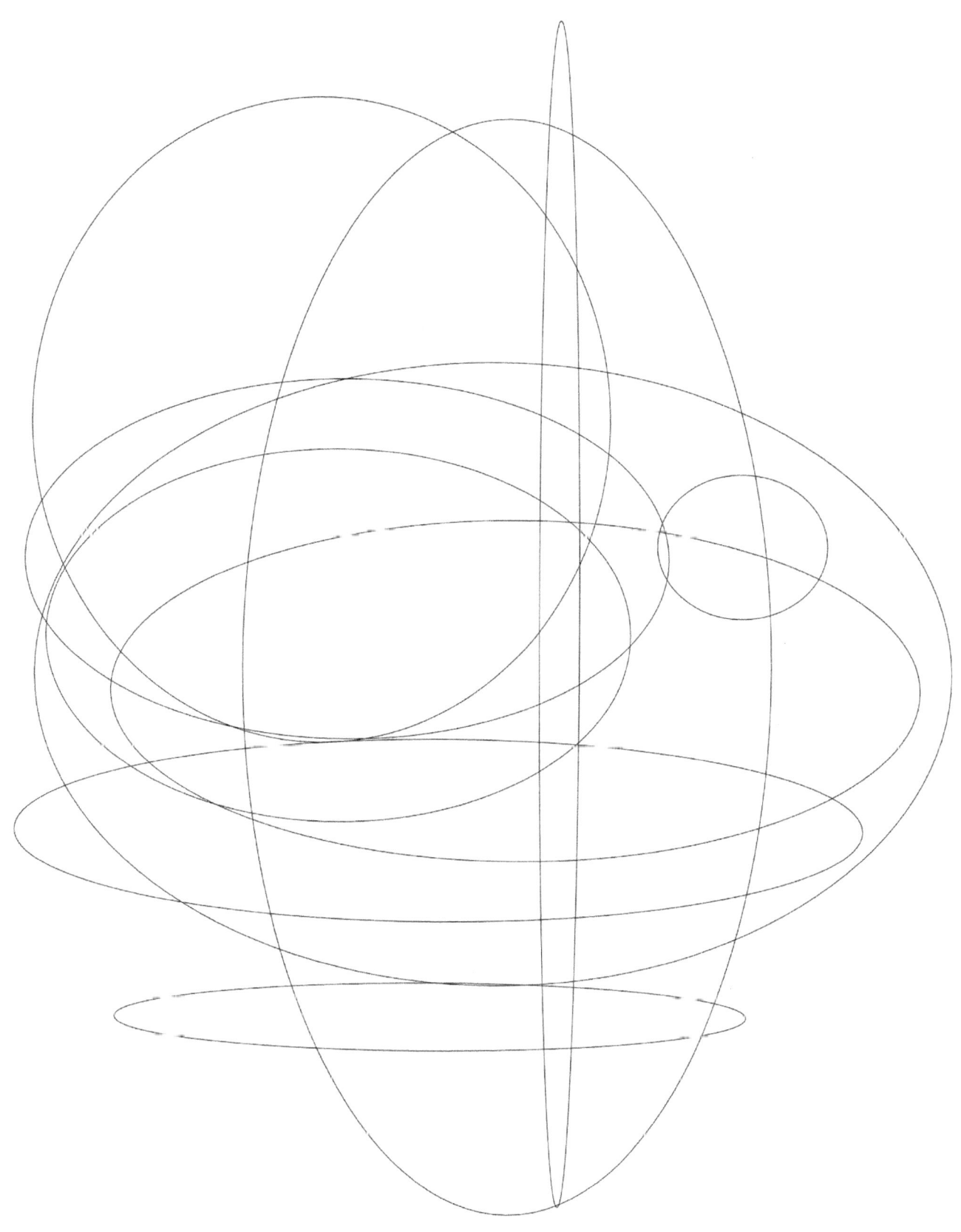

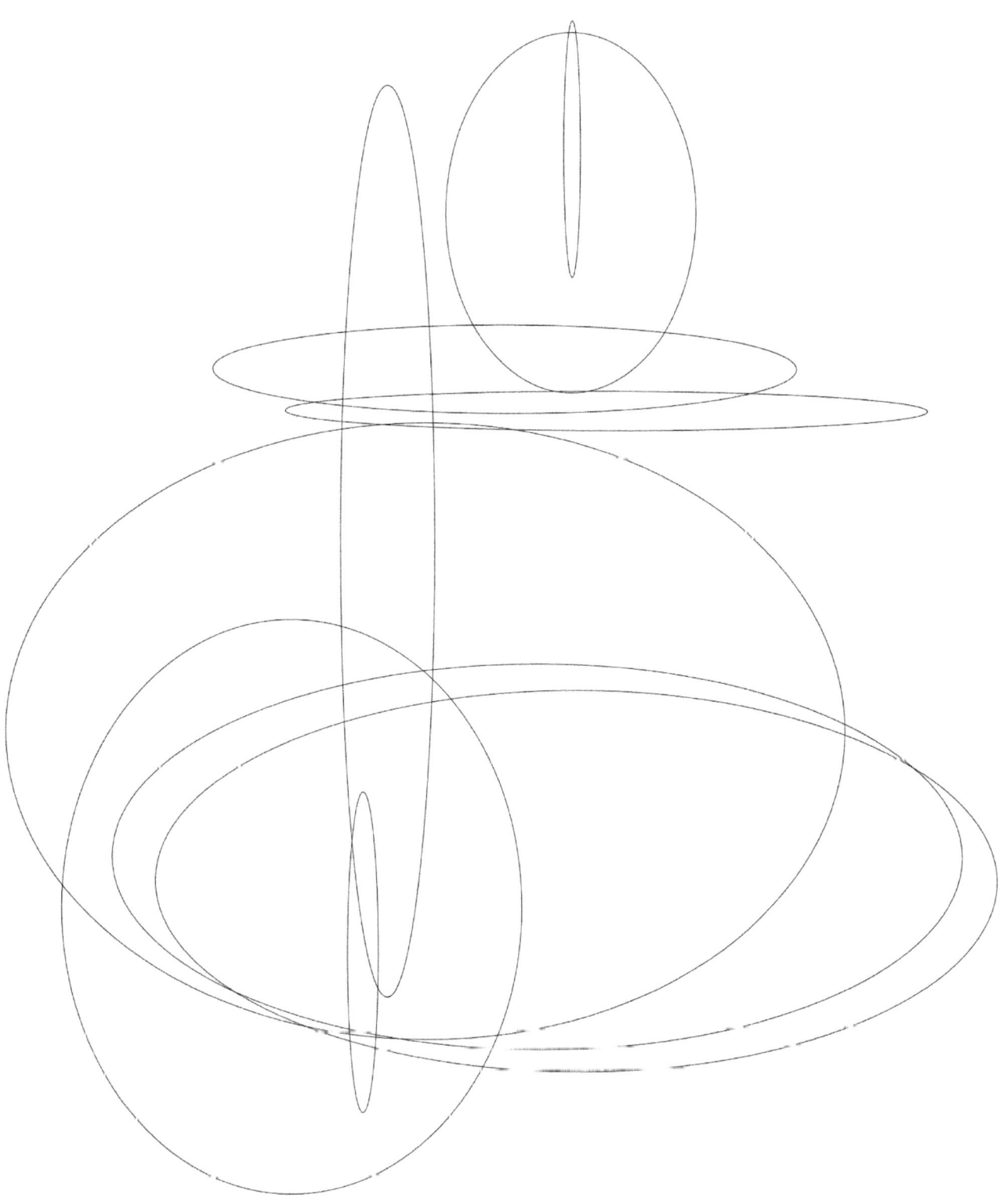

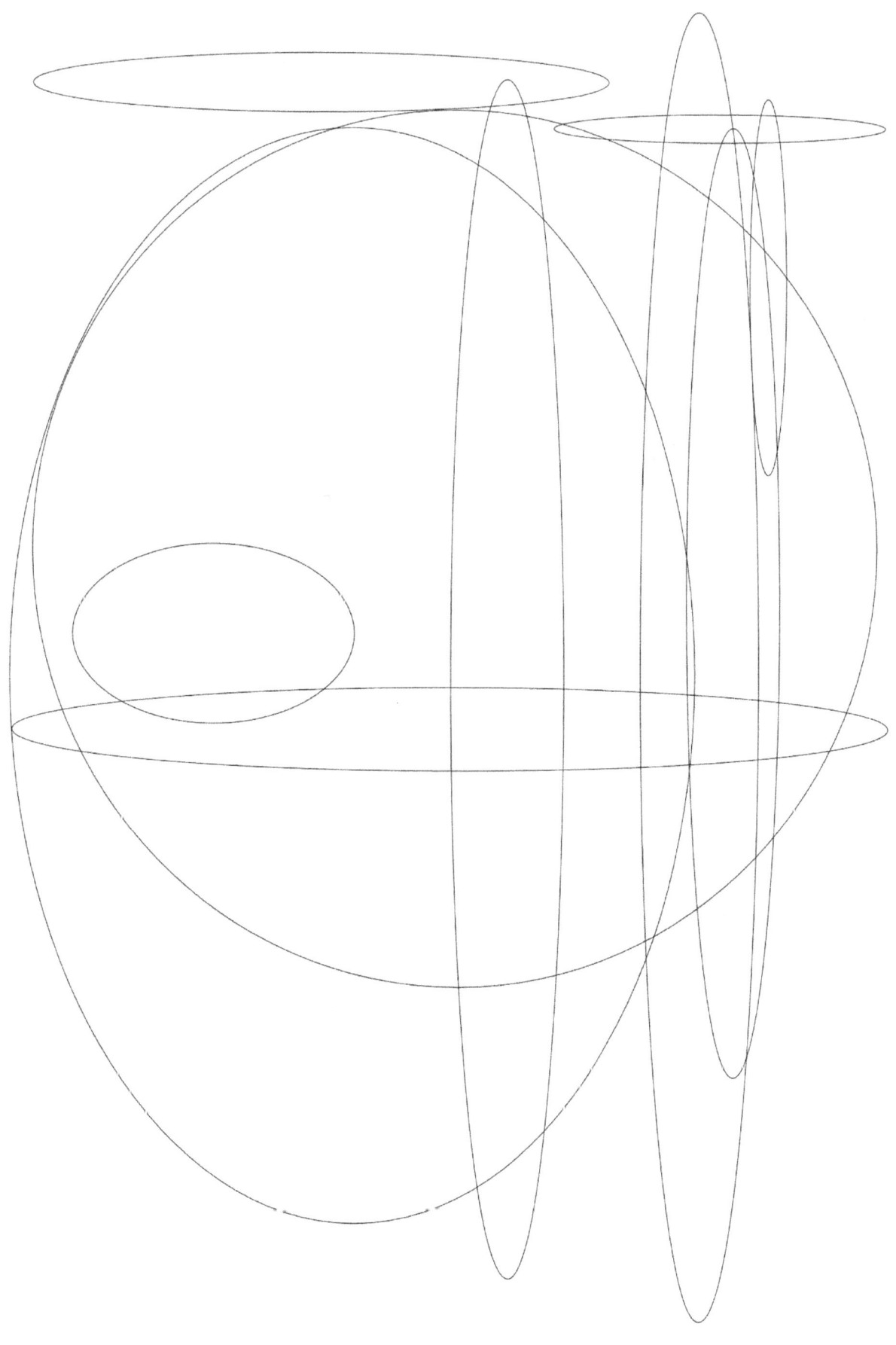

J. Mummey

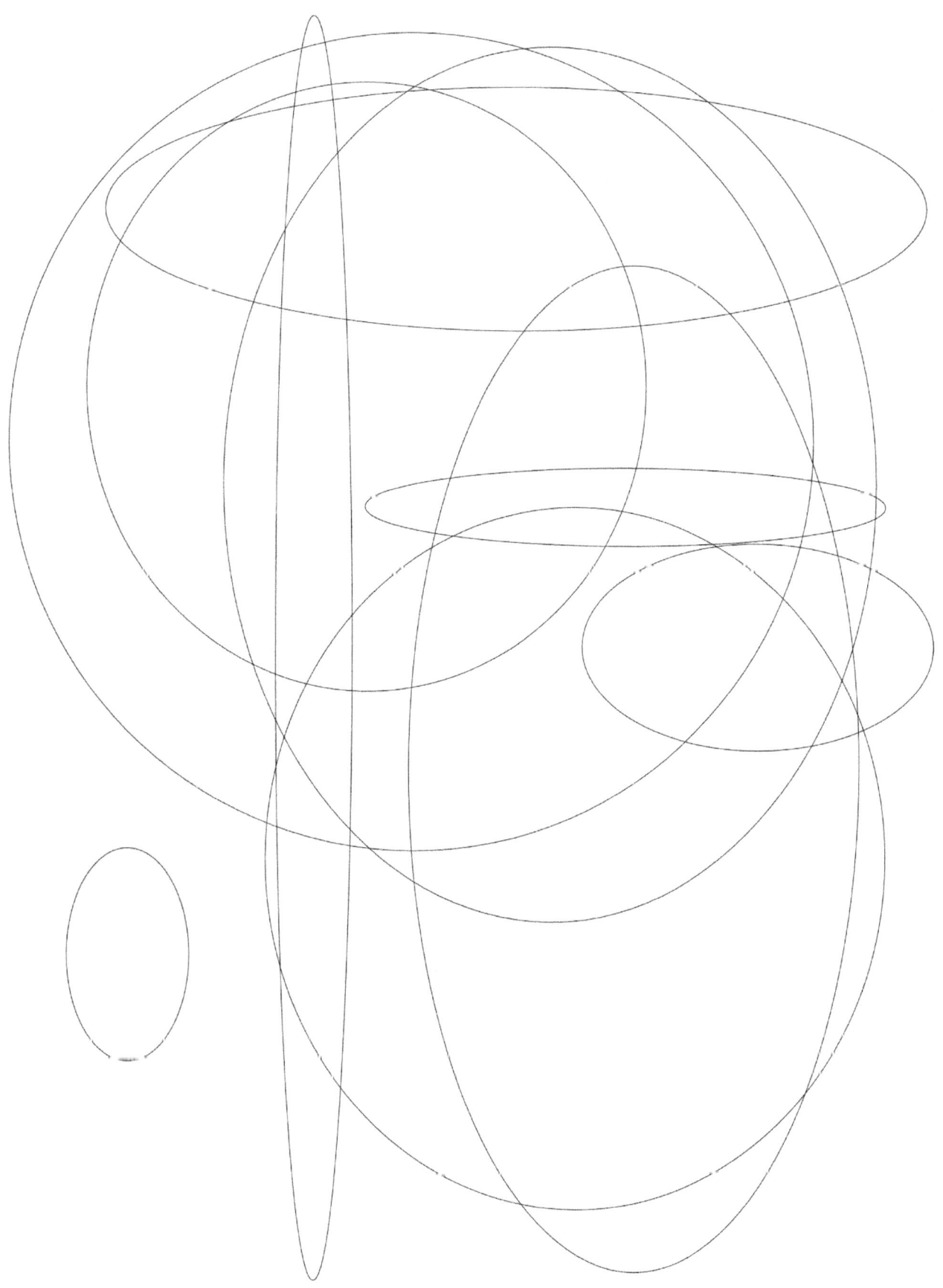

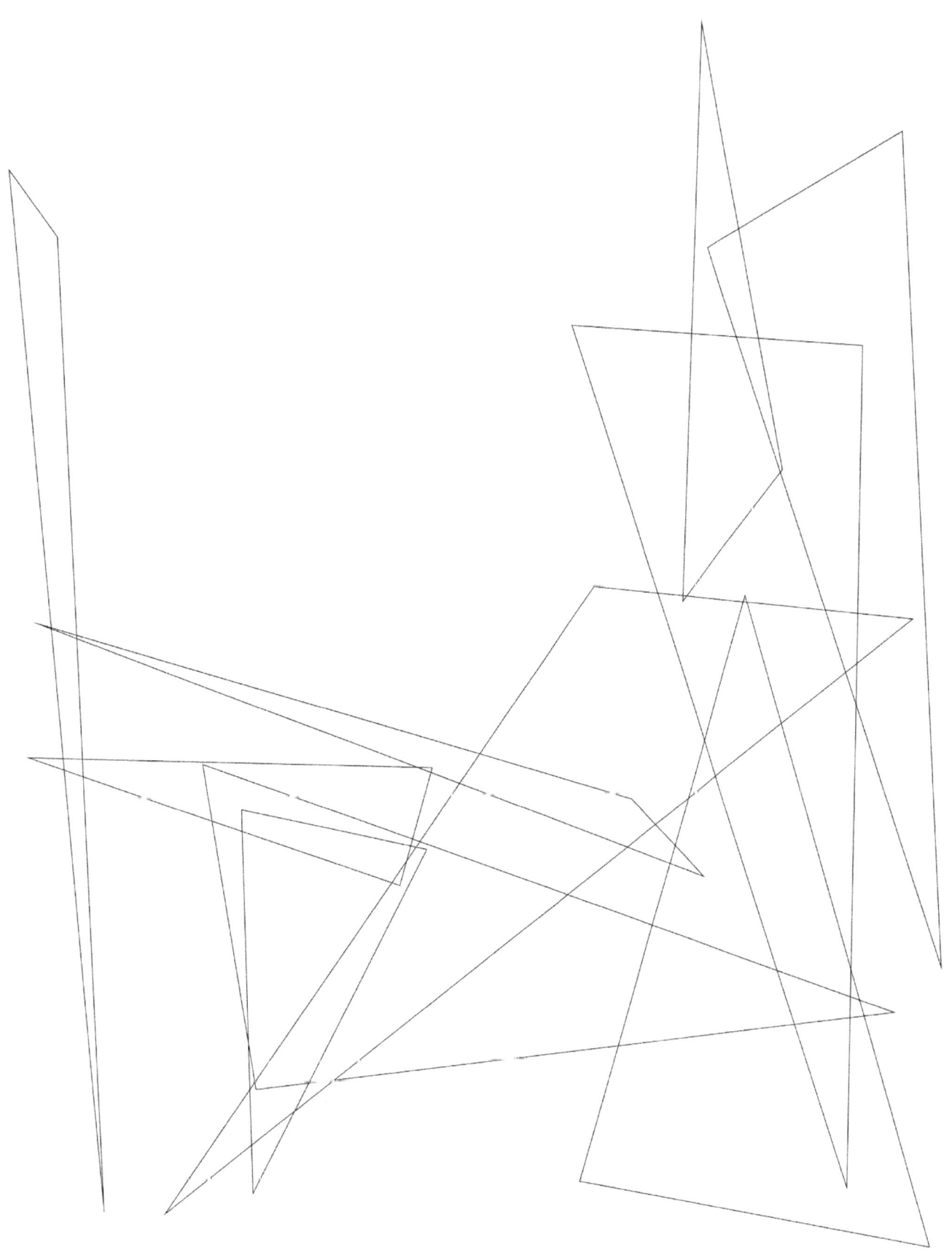

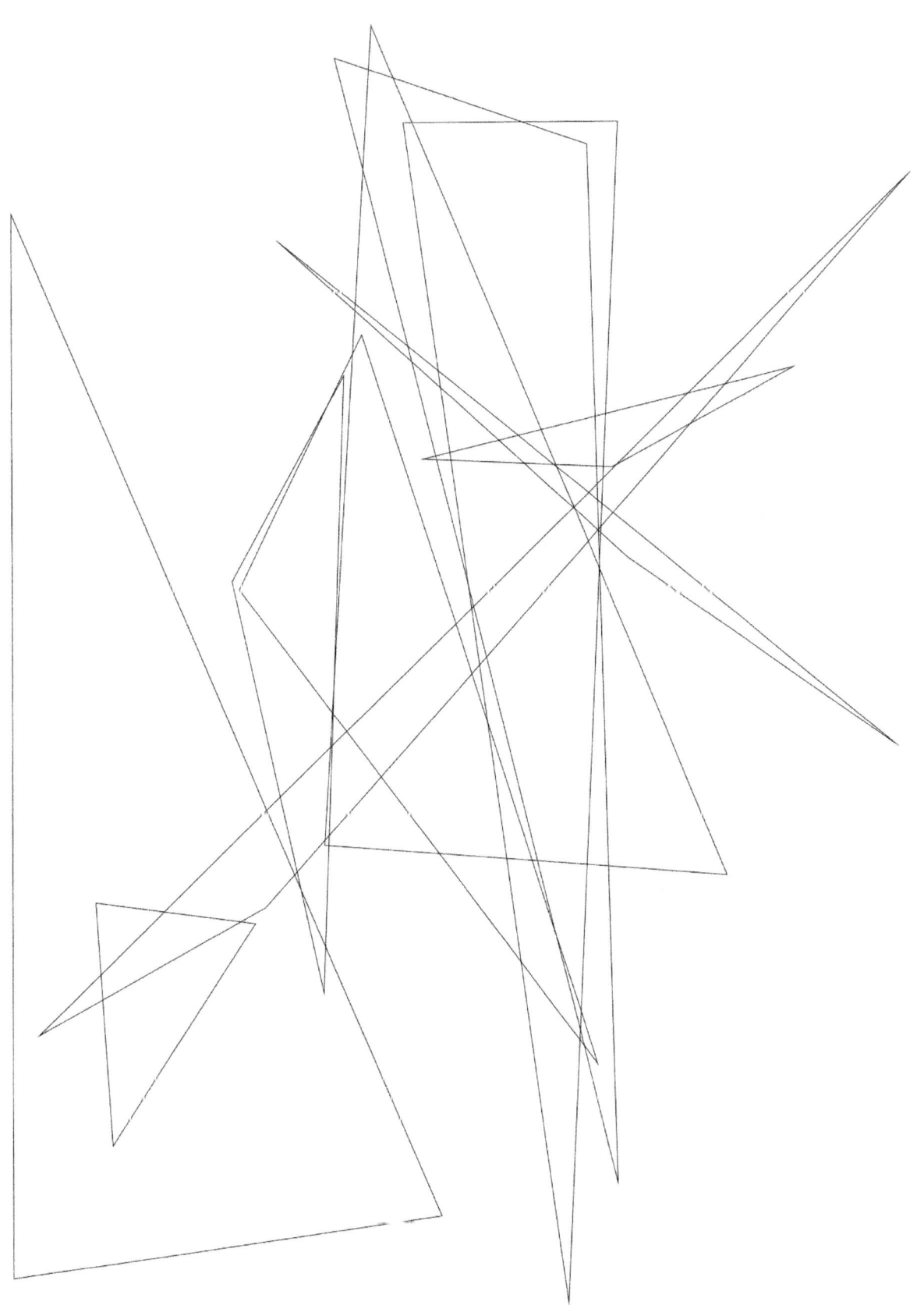

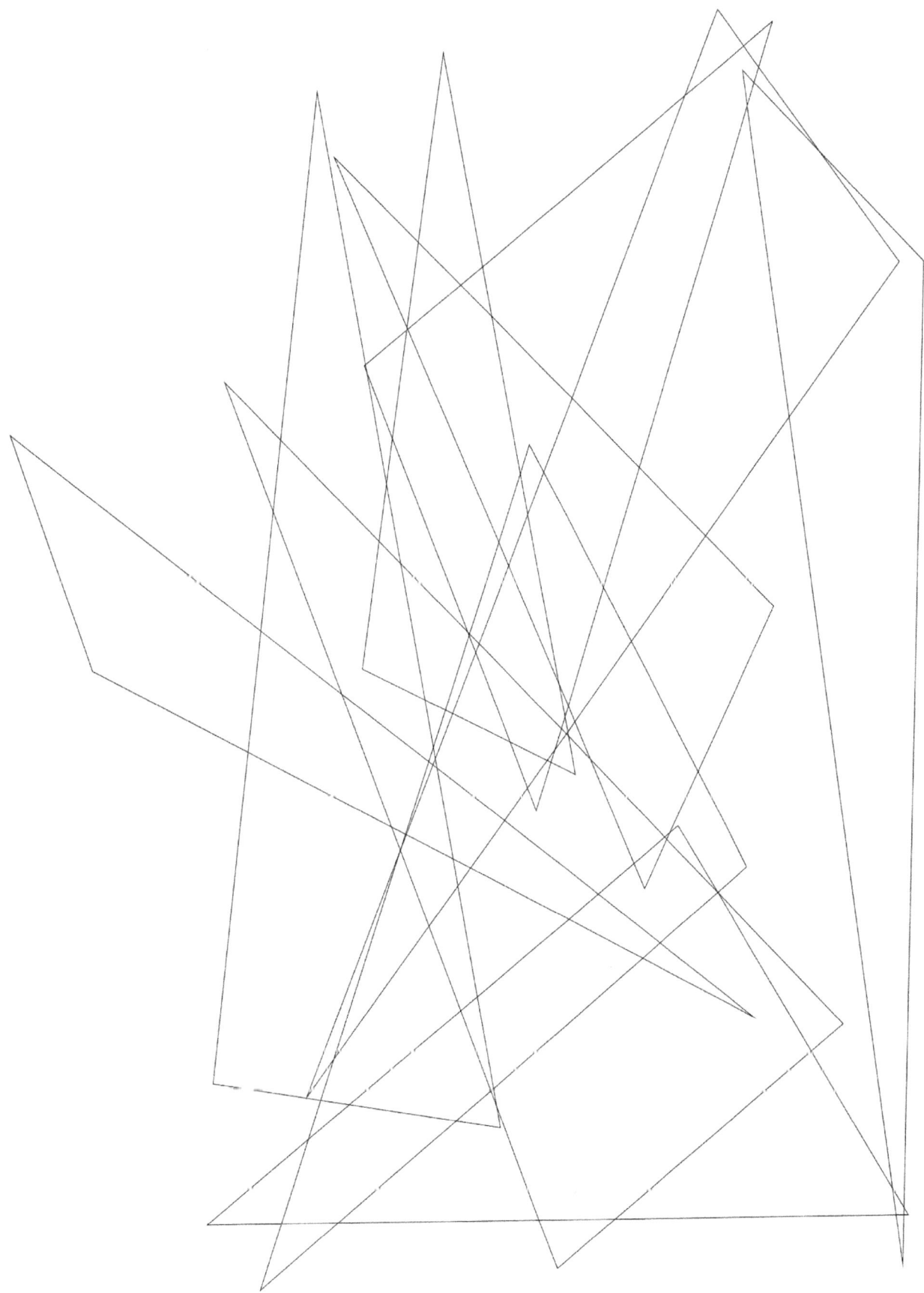

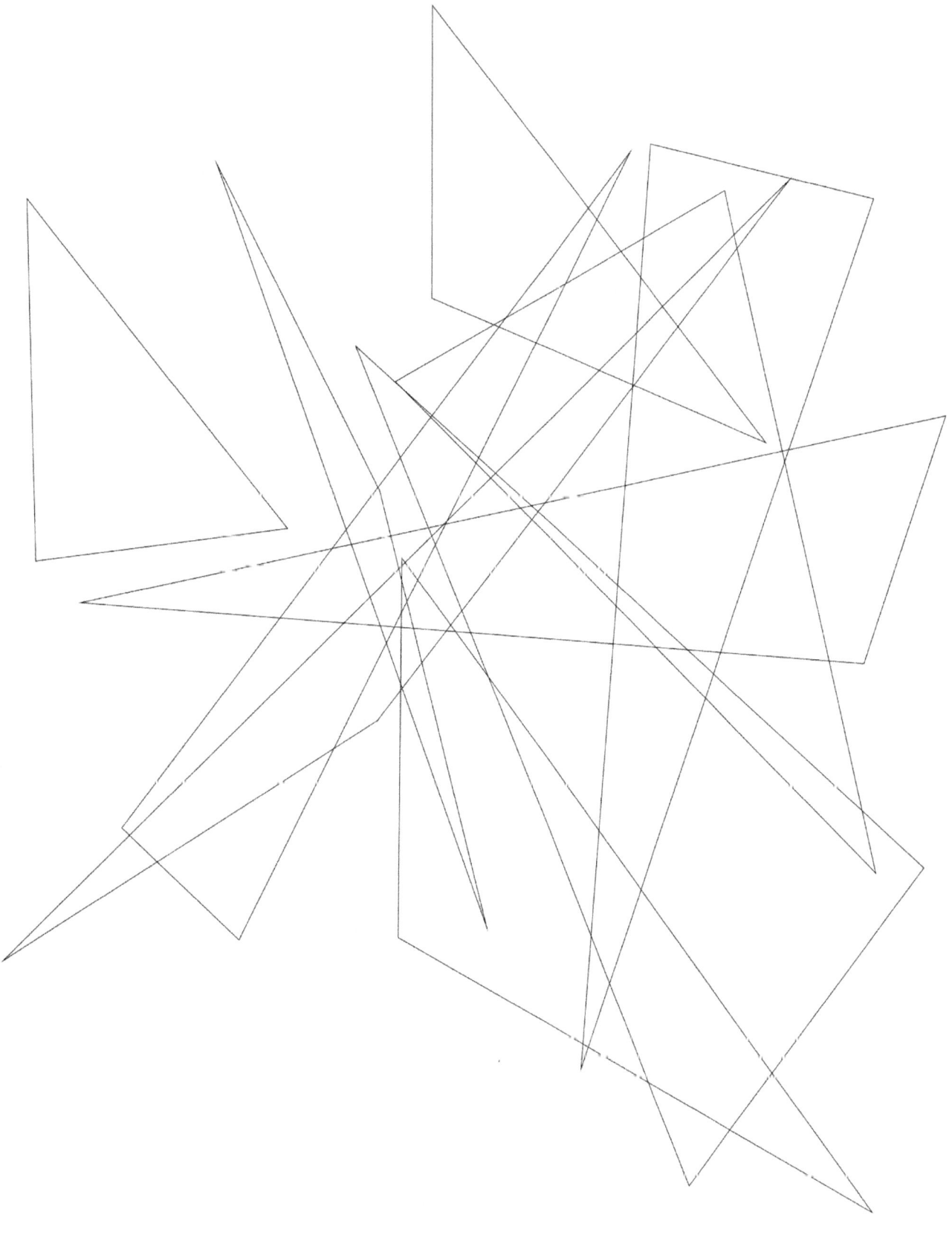

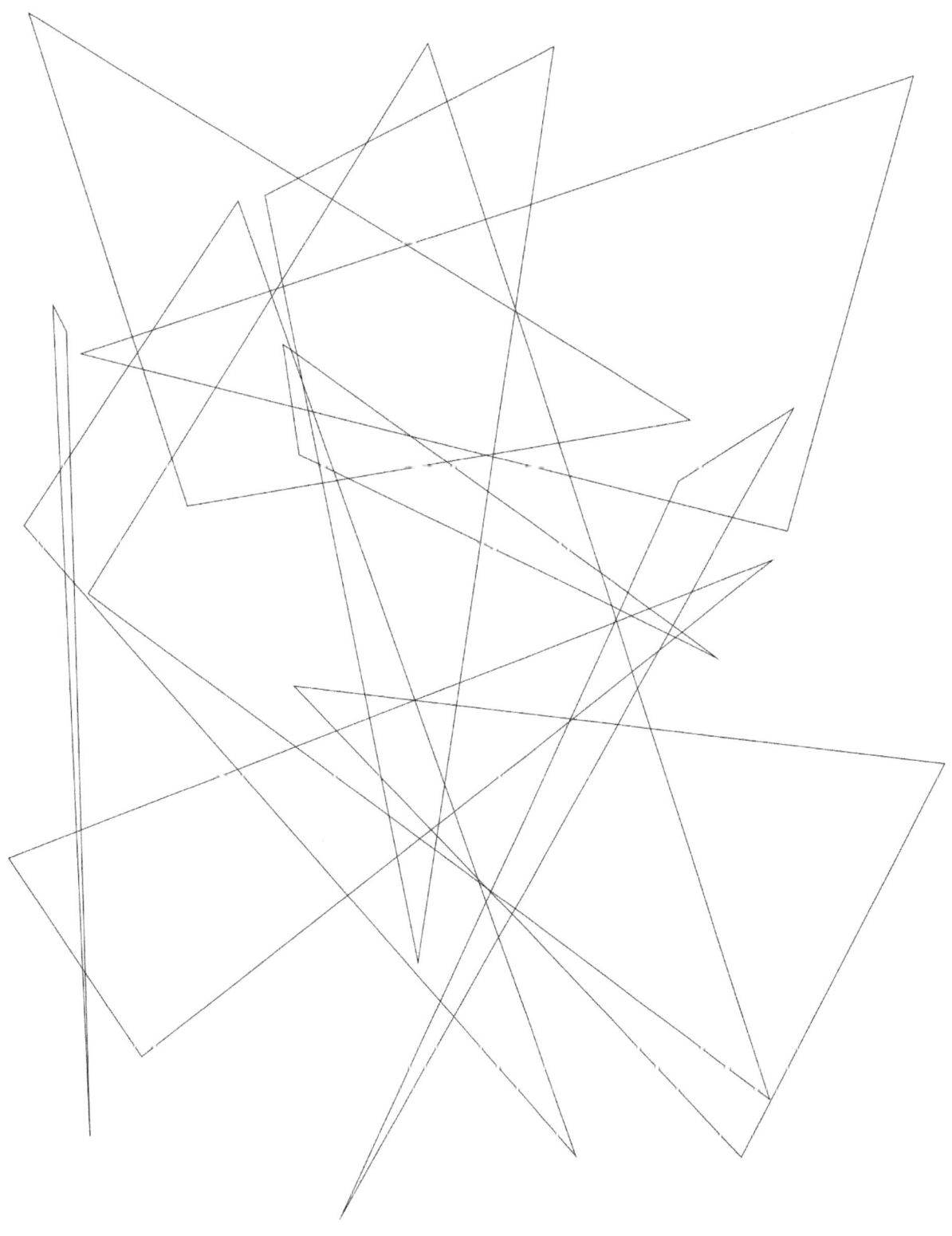

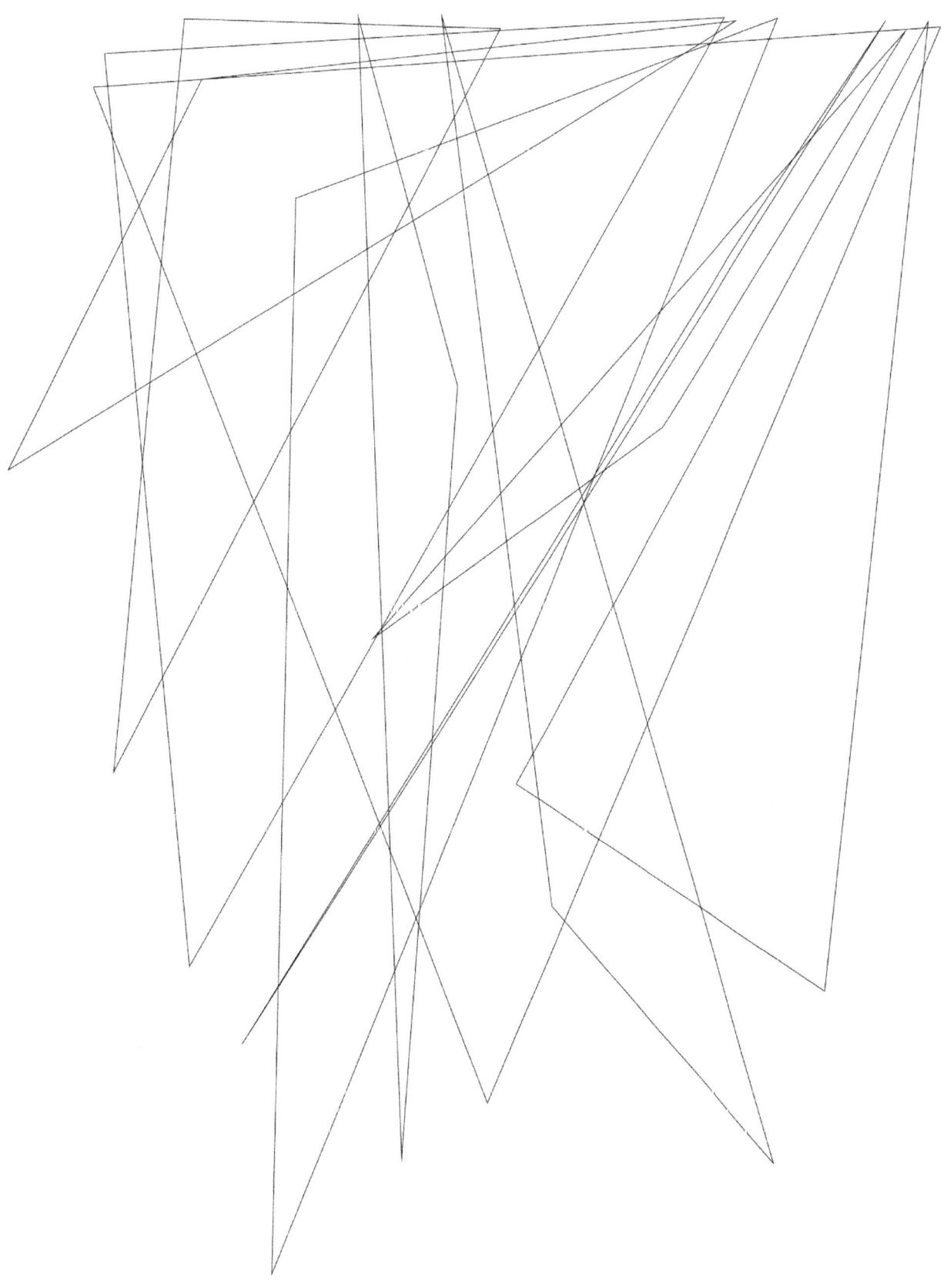

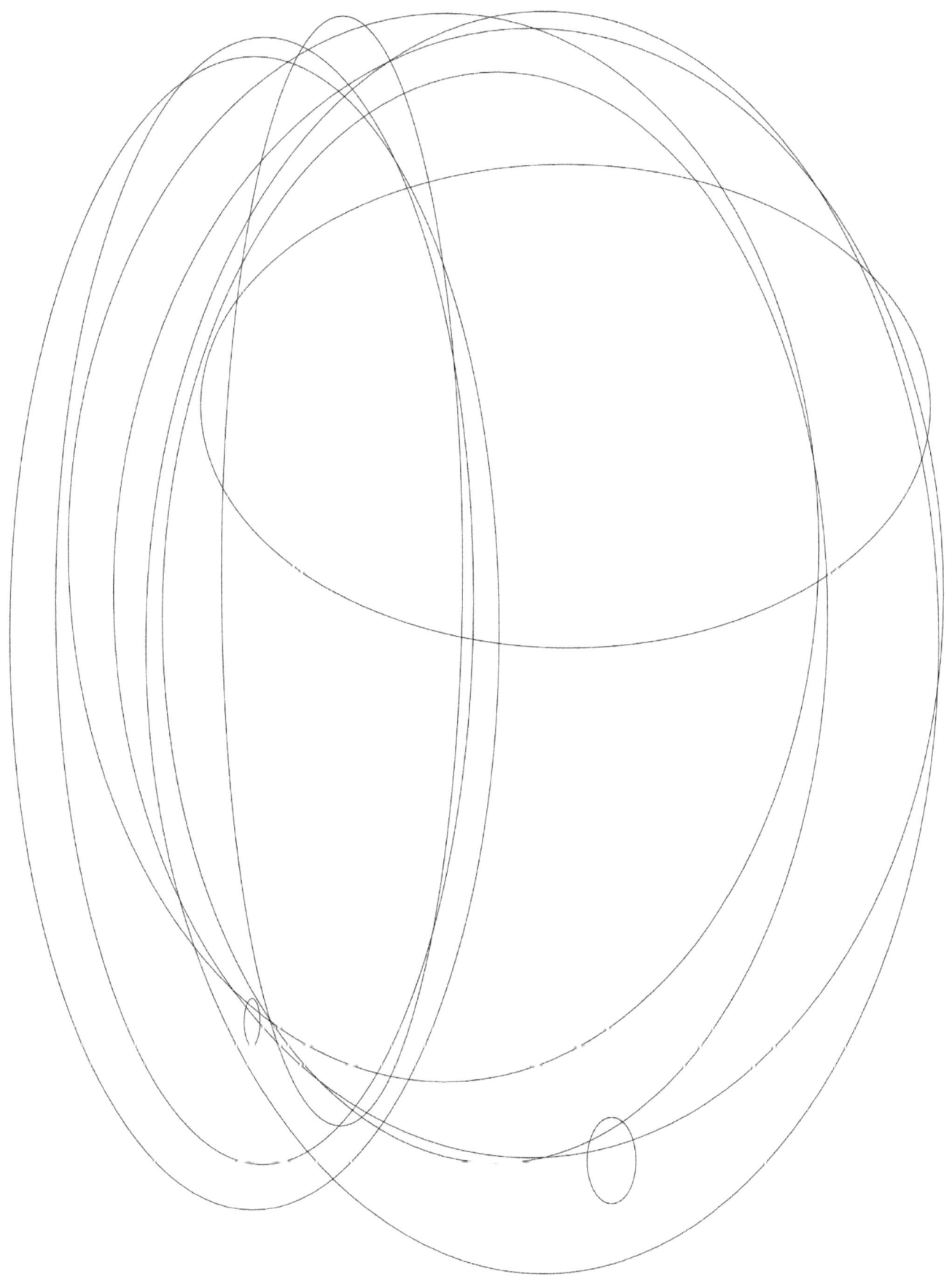

J. Mummey

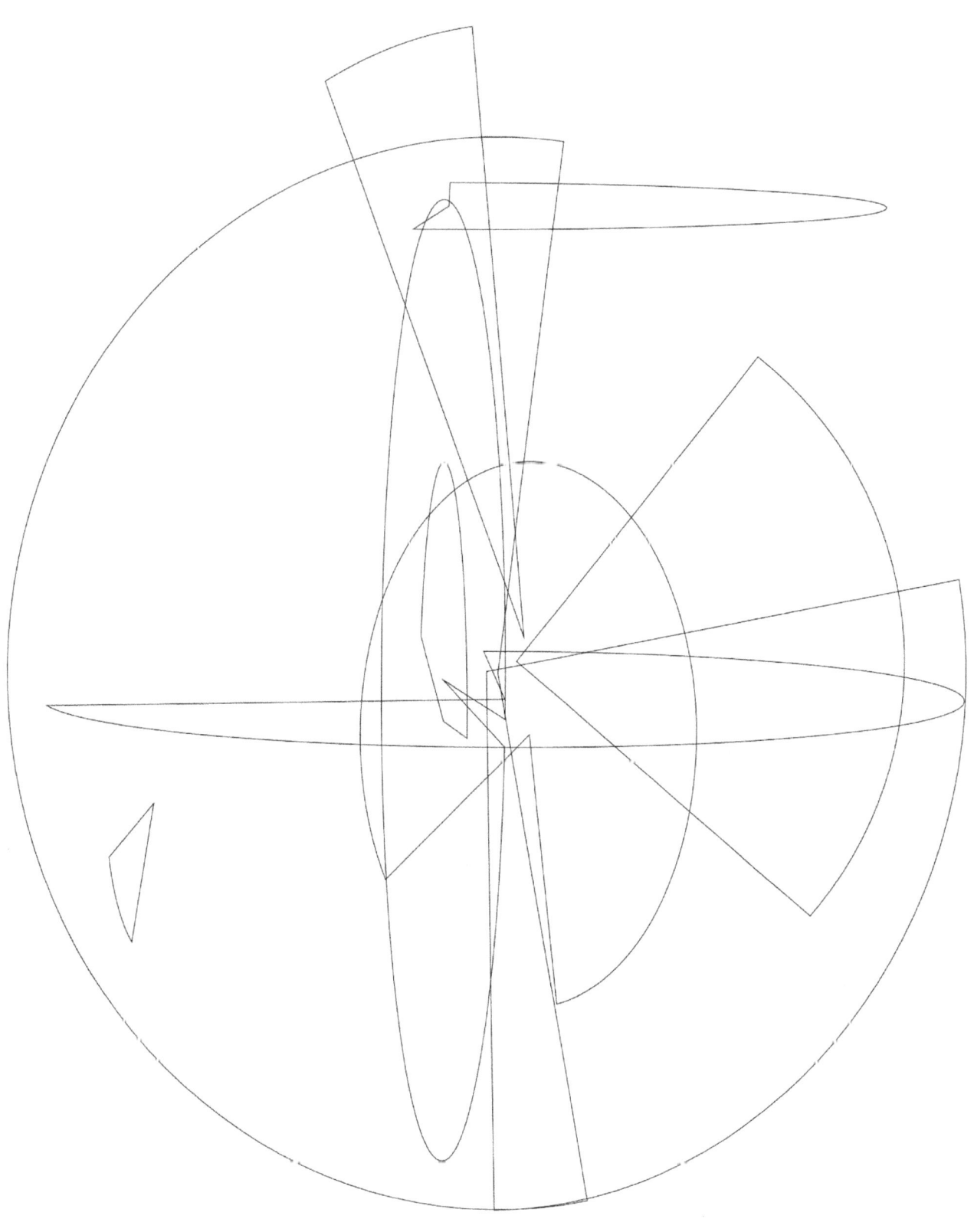

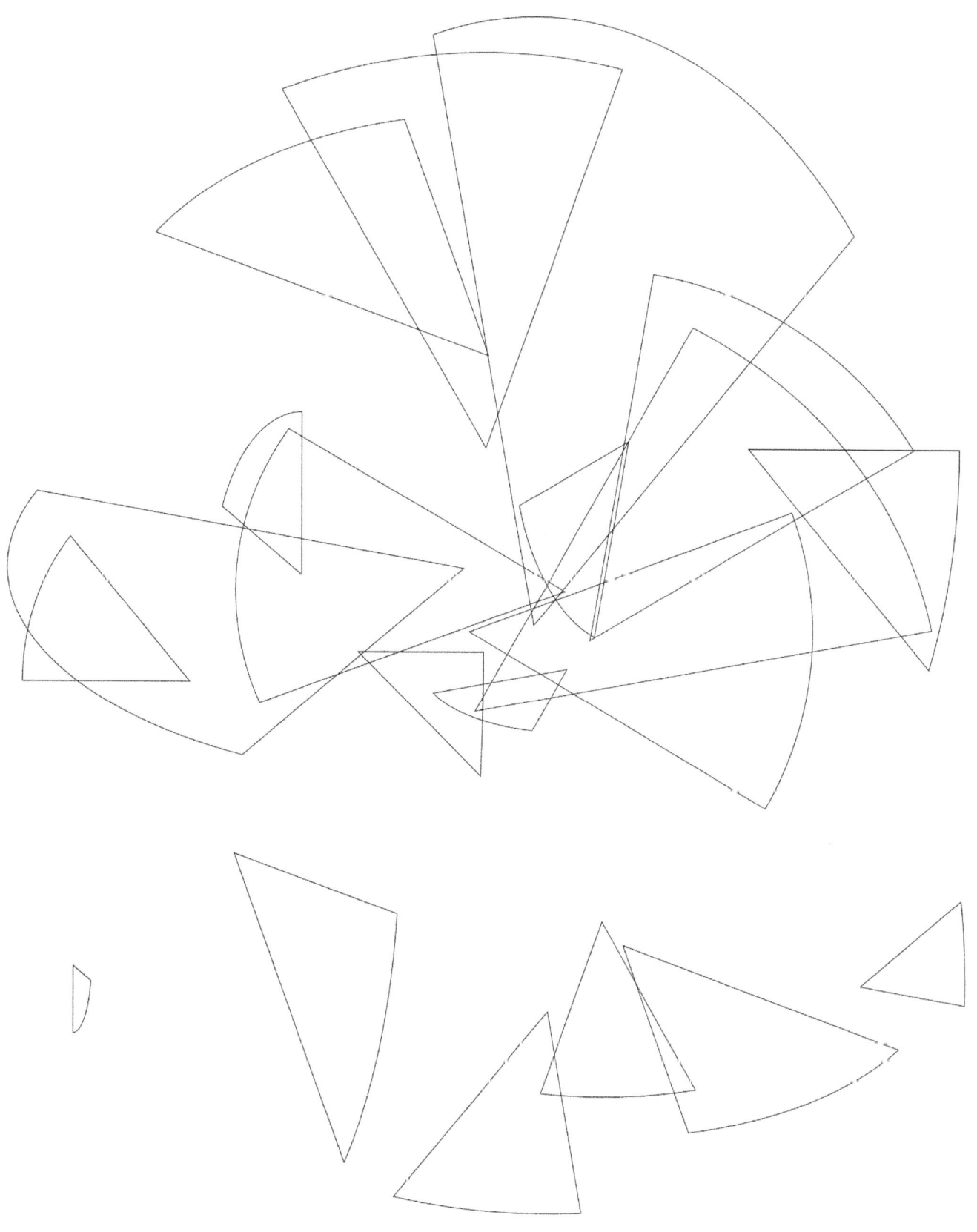

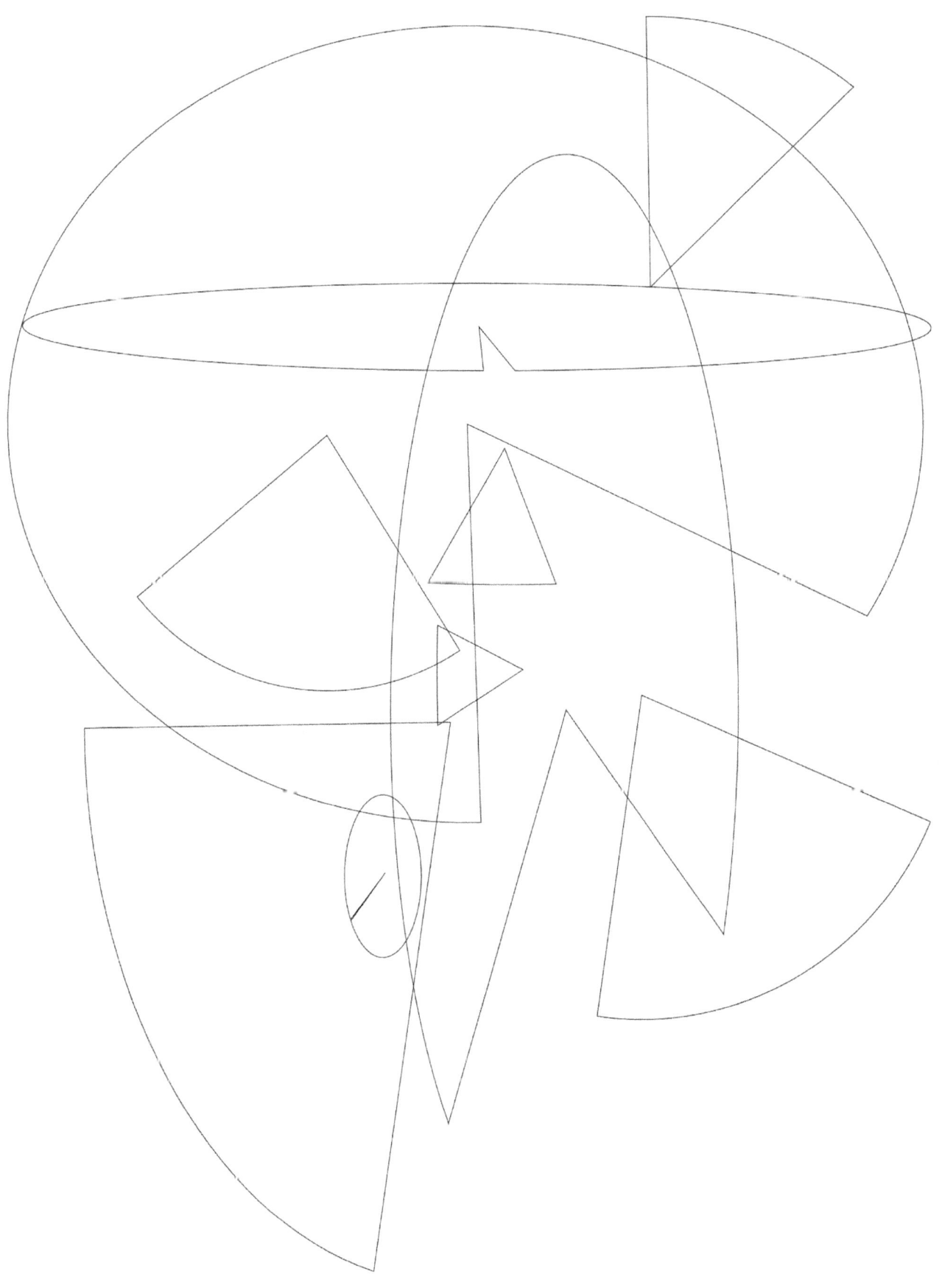

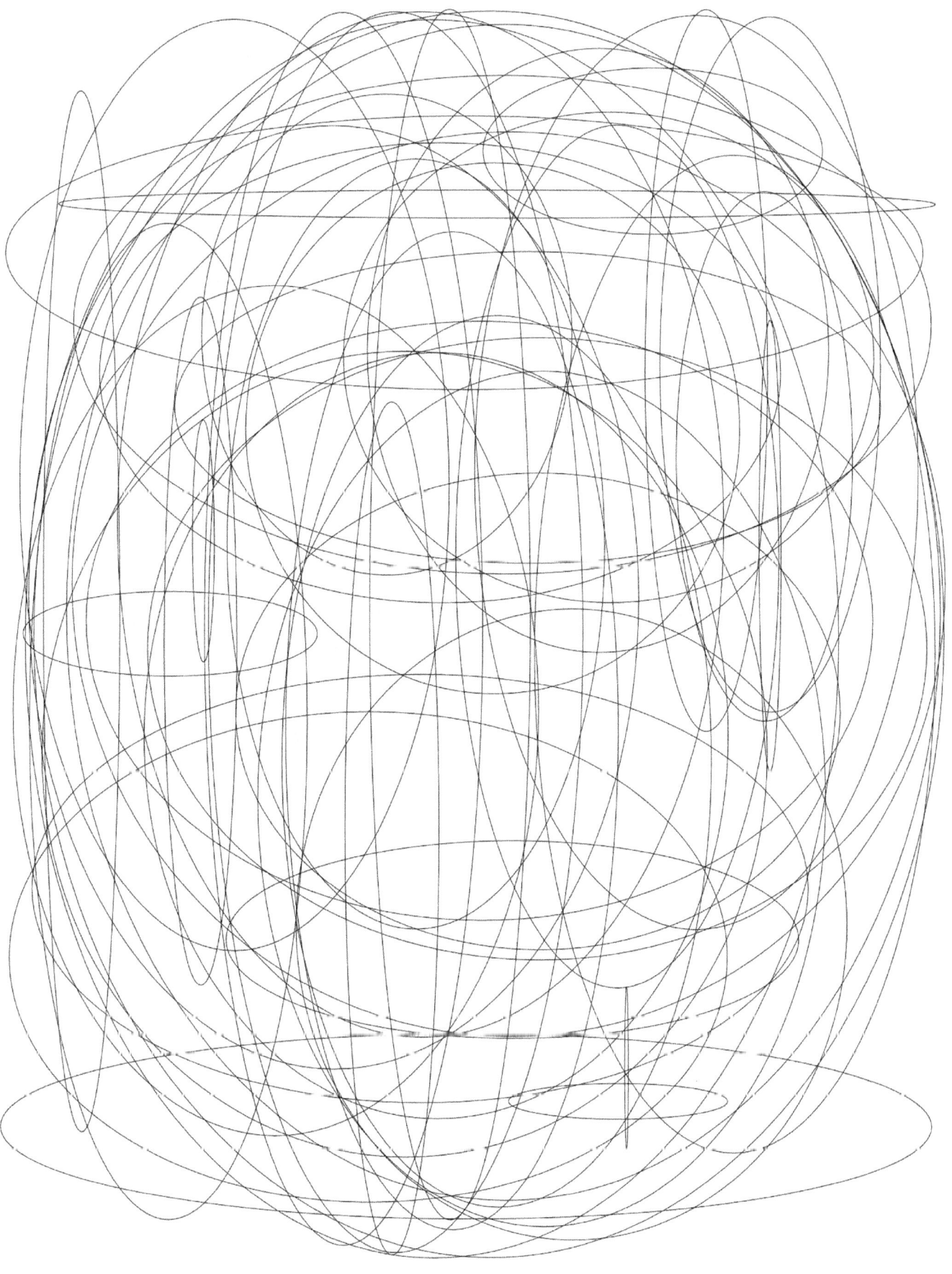

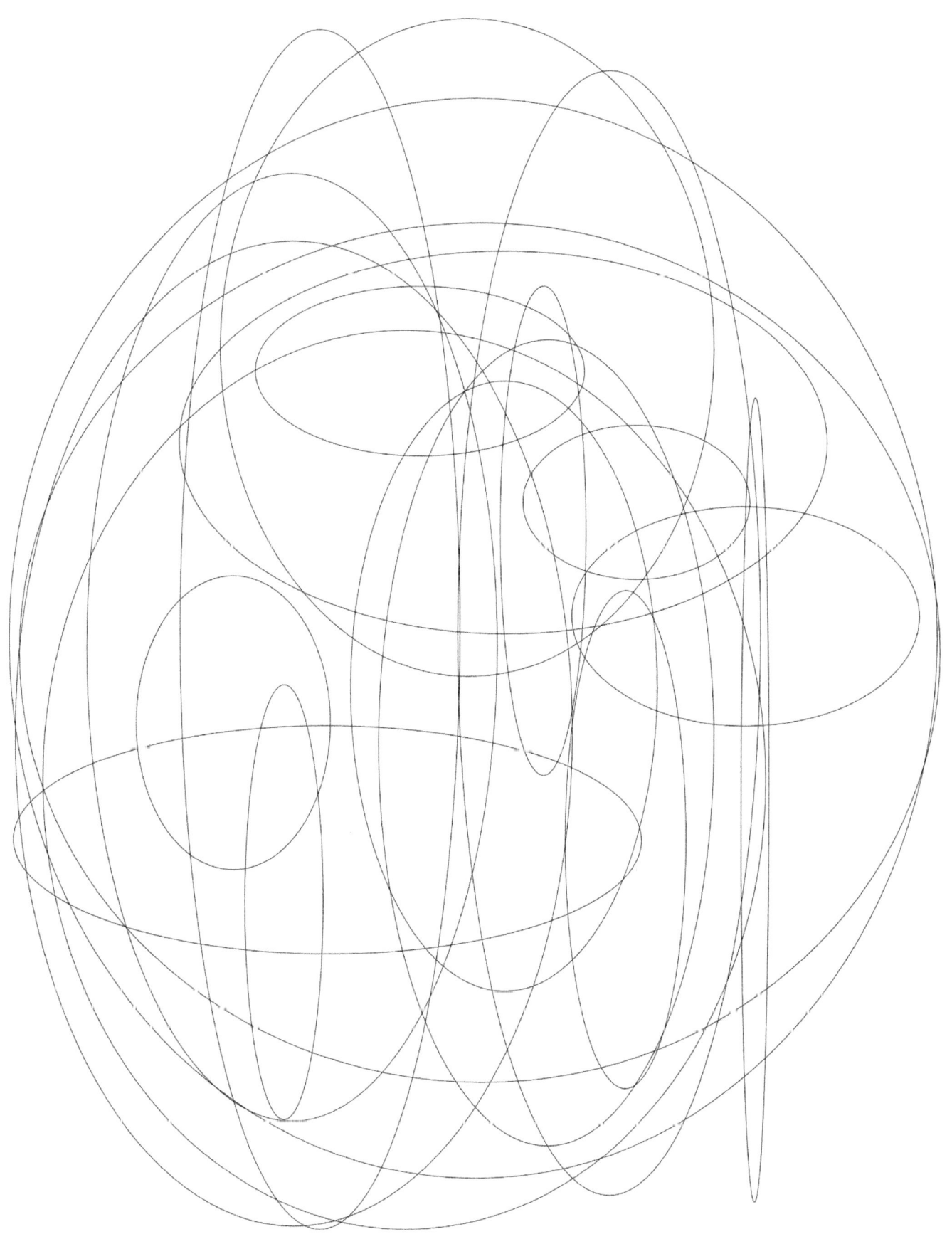

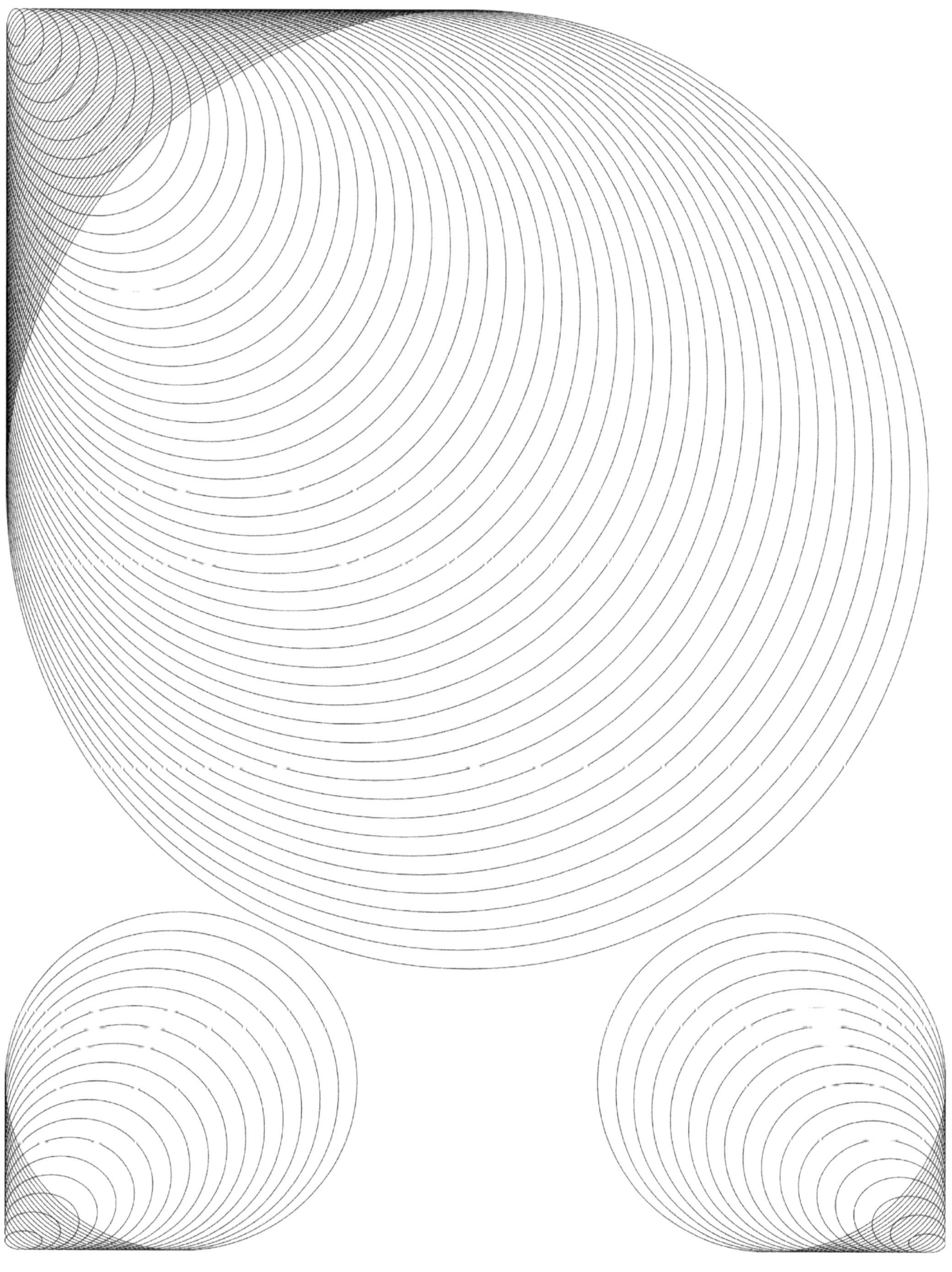

.

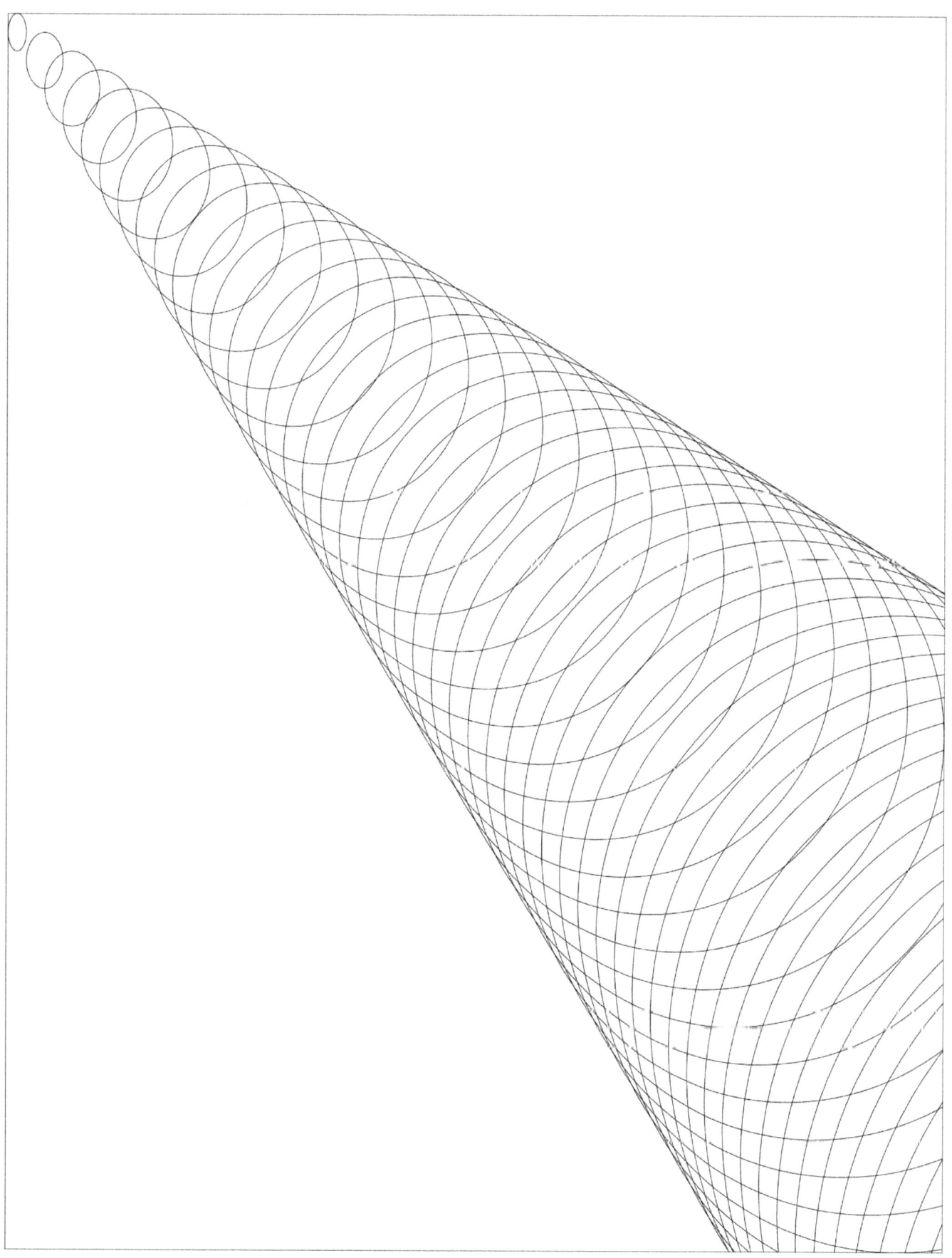

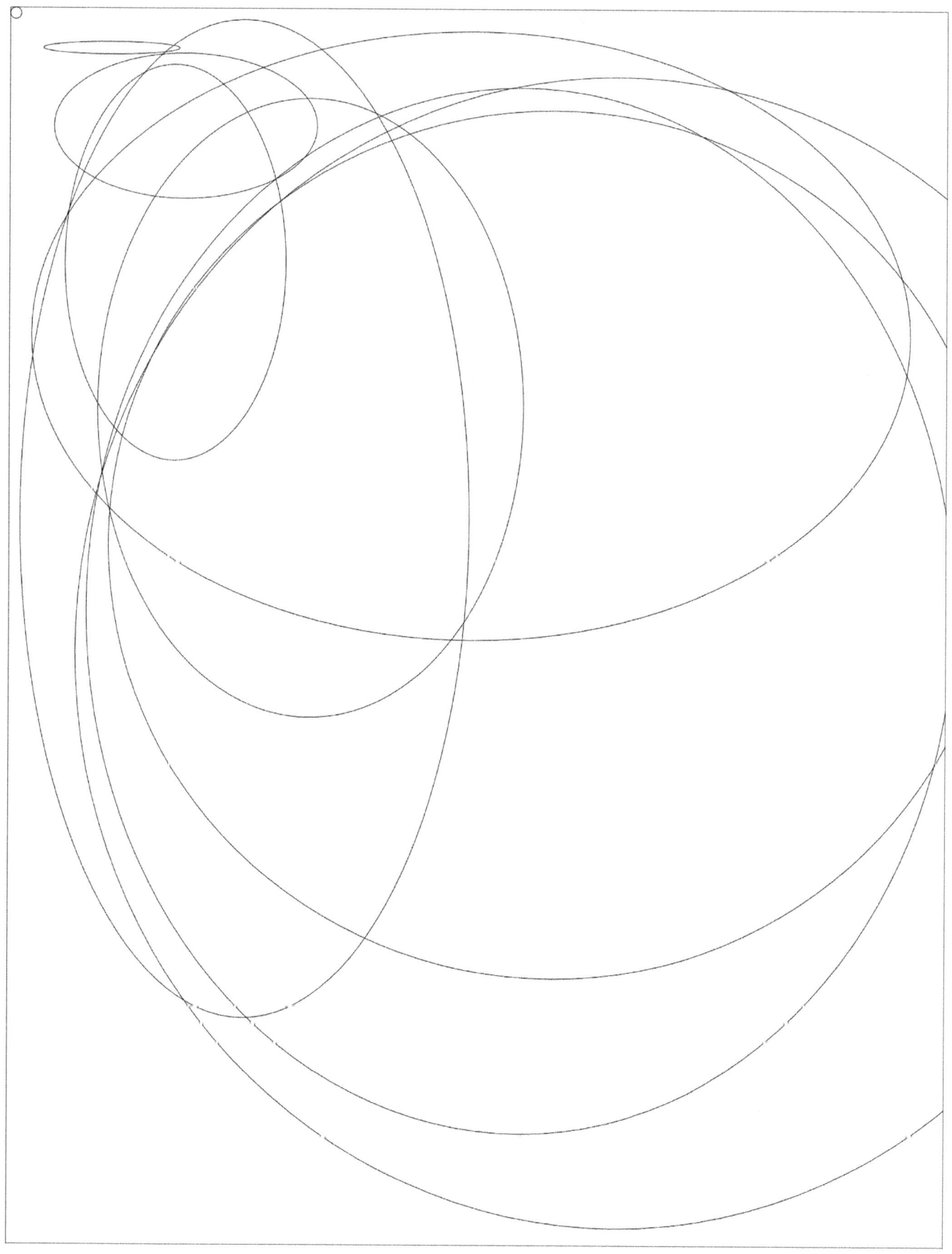

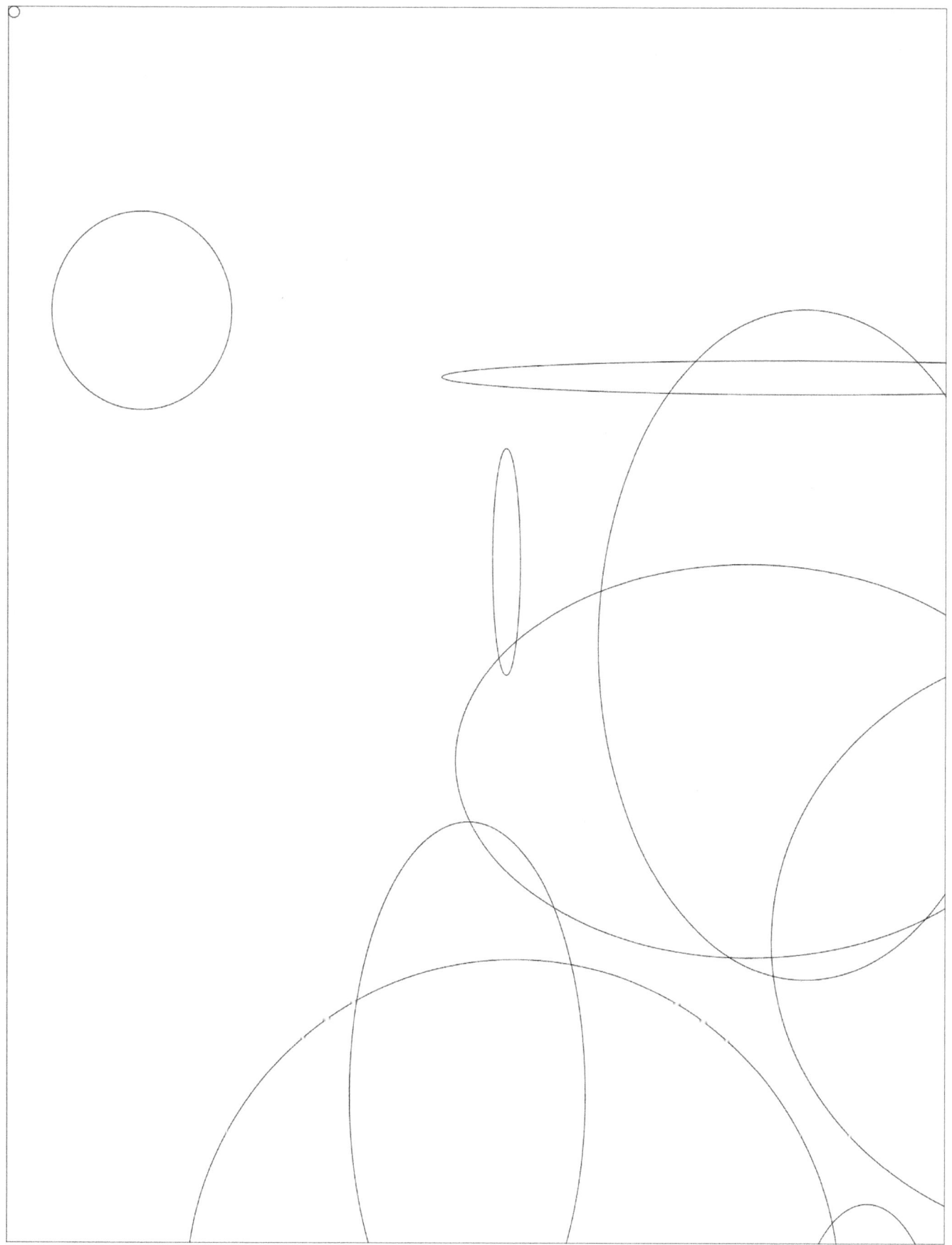

J. Mummey

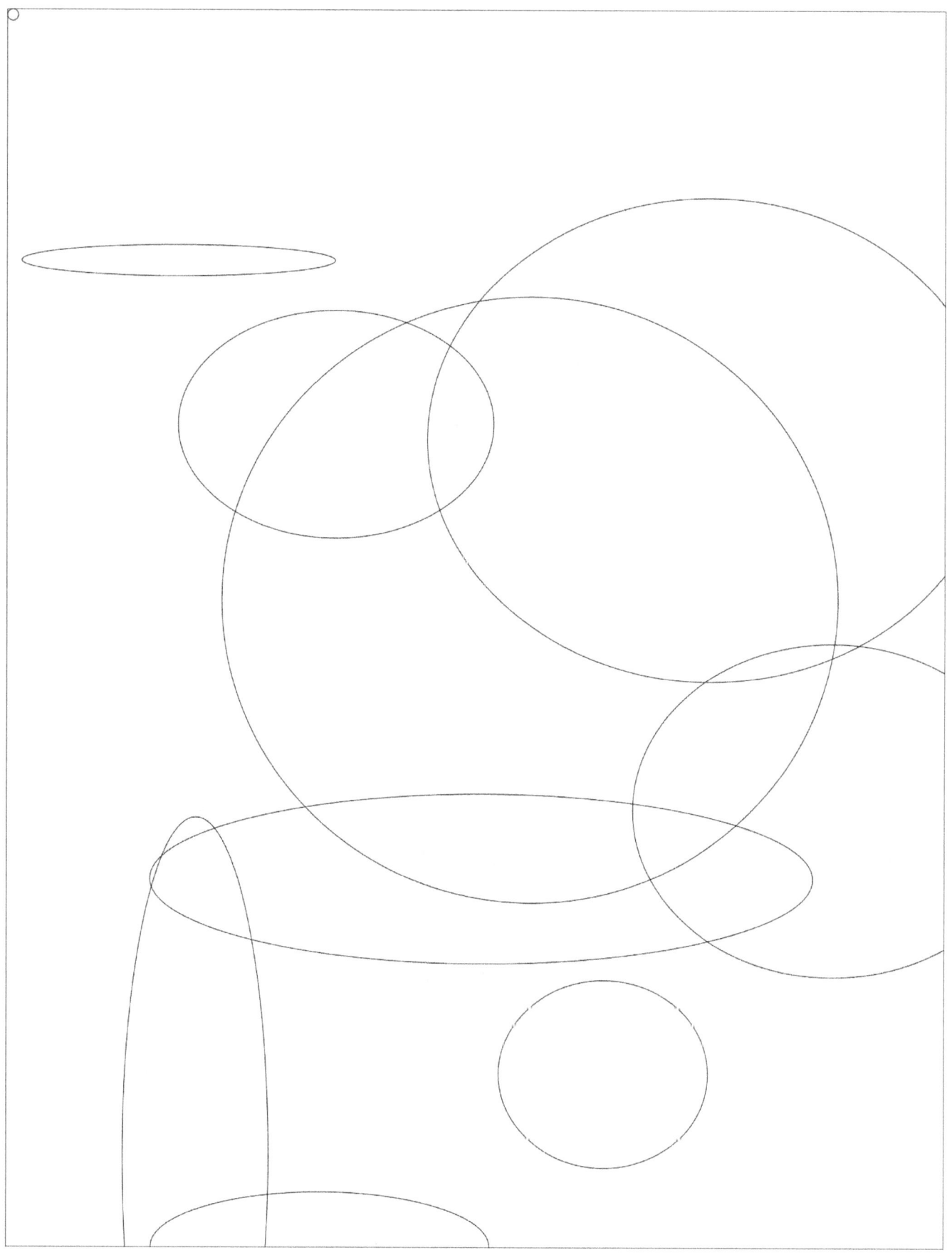

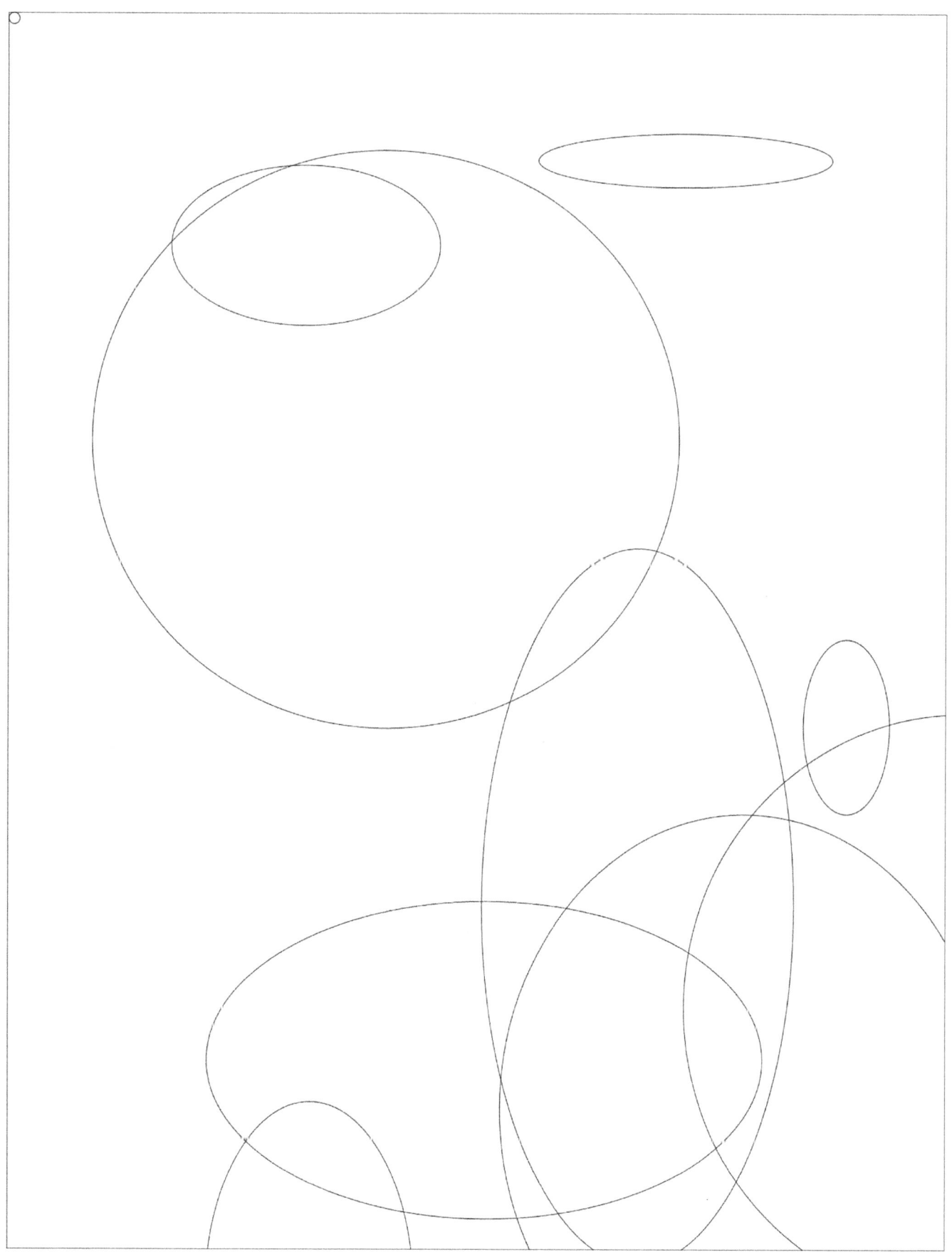

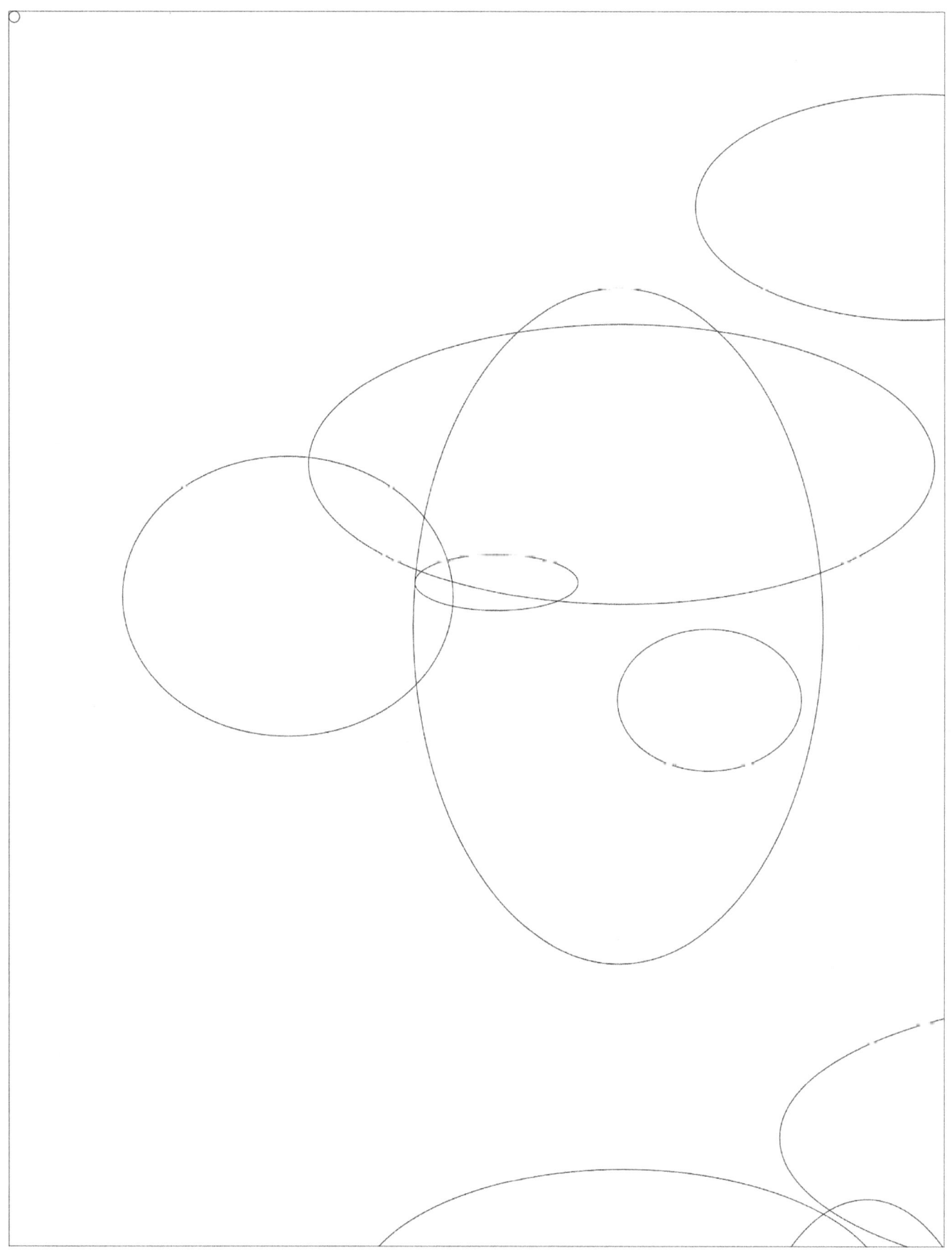

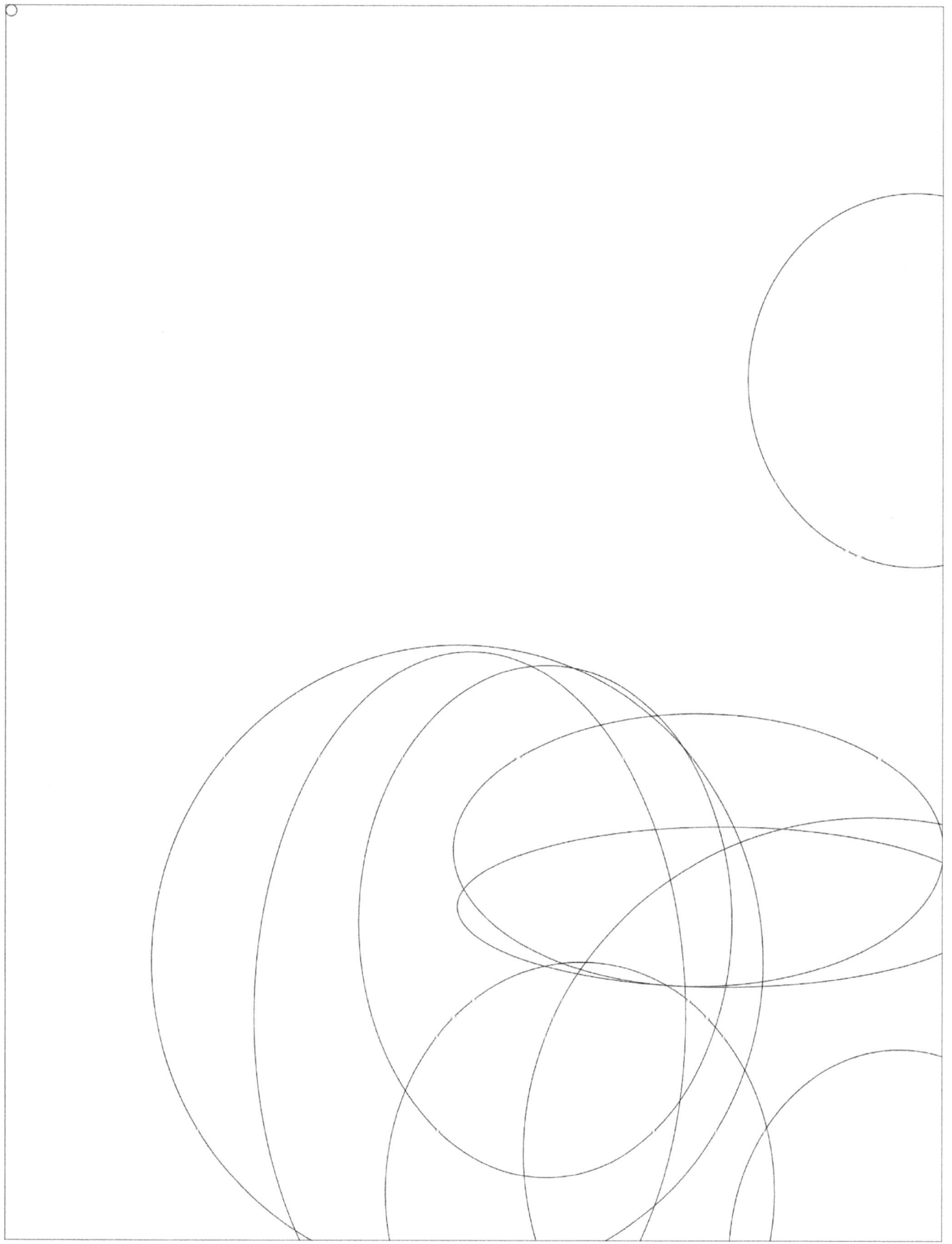

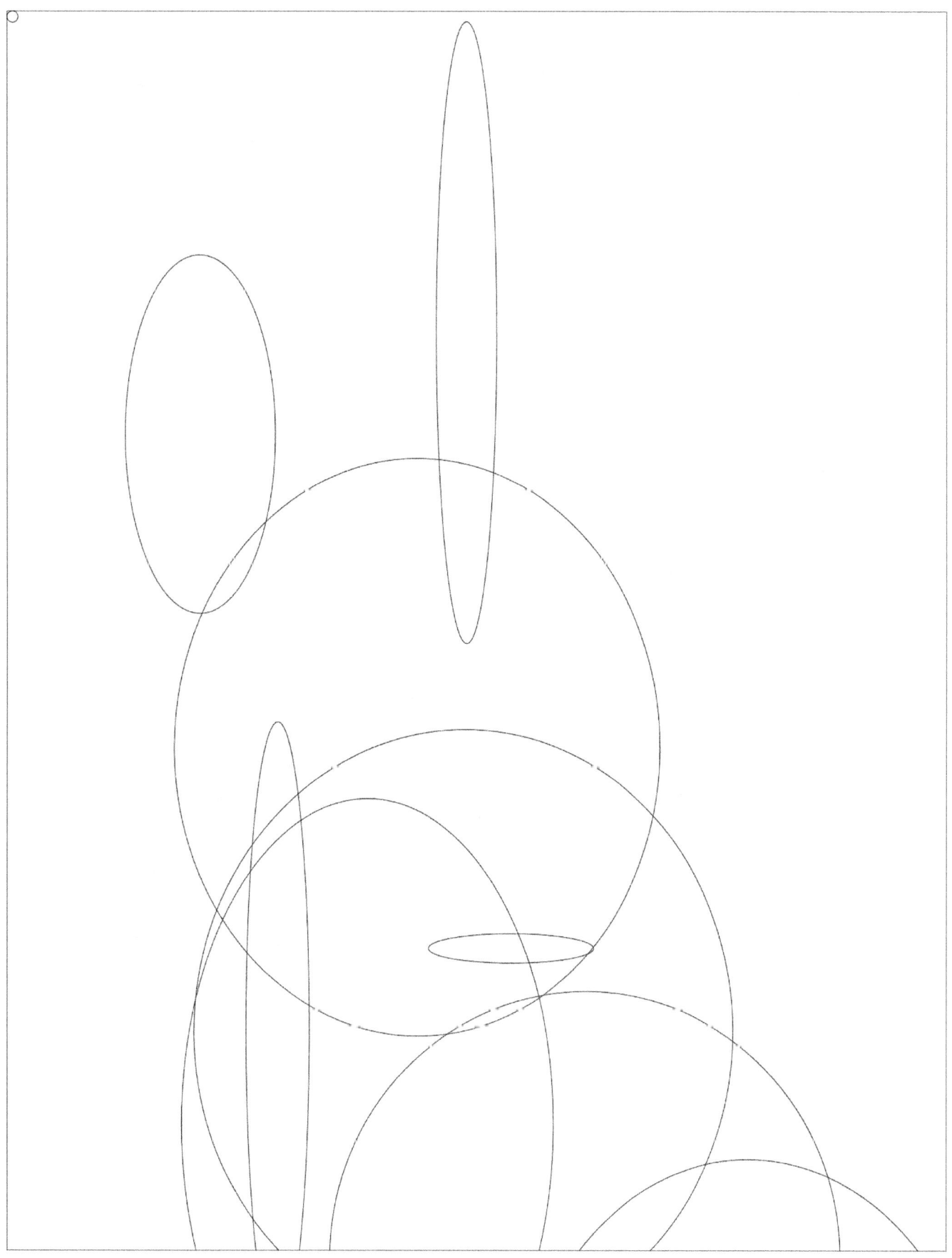

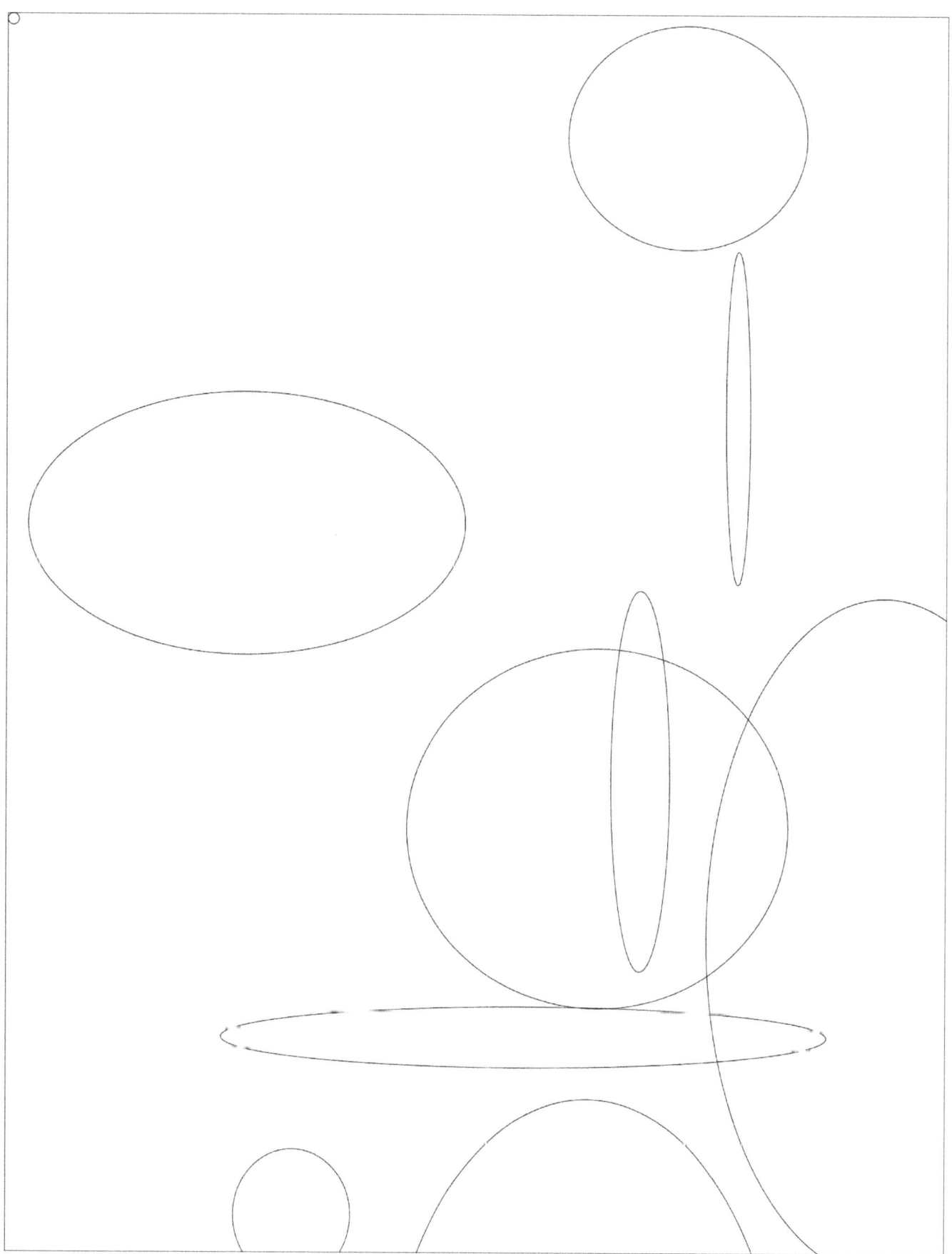

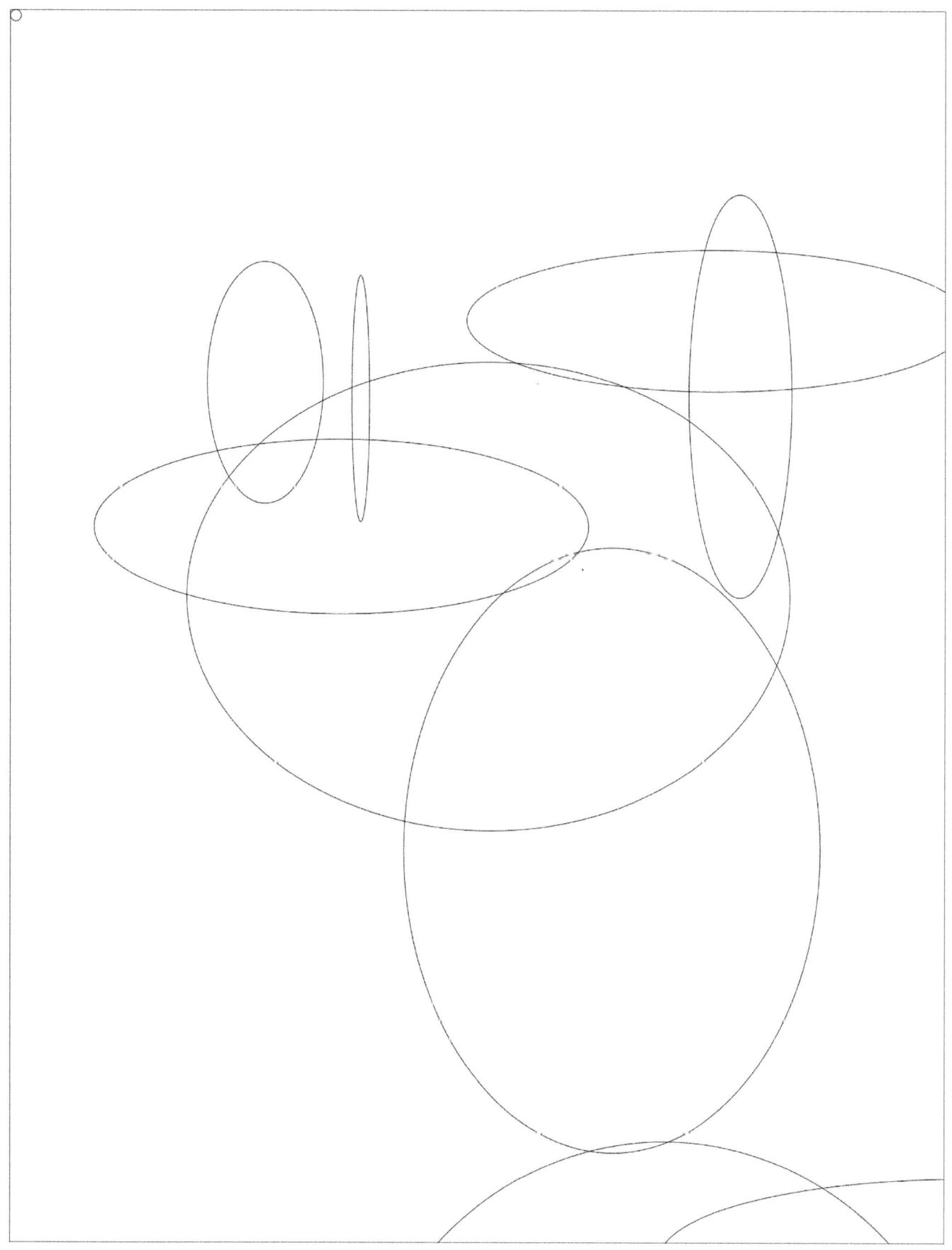

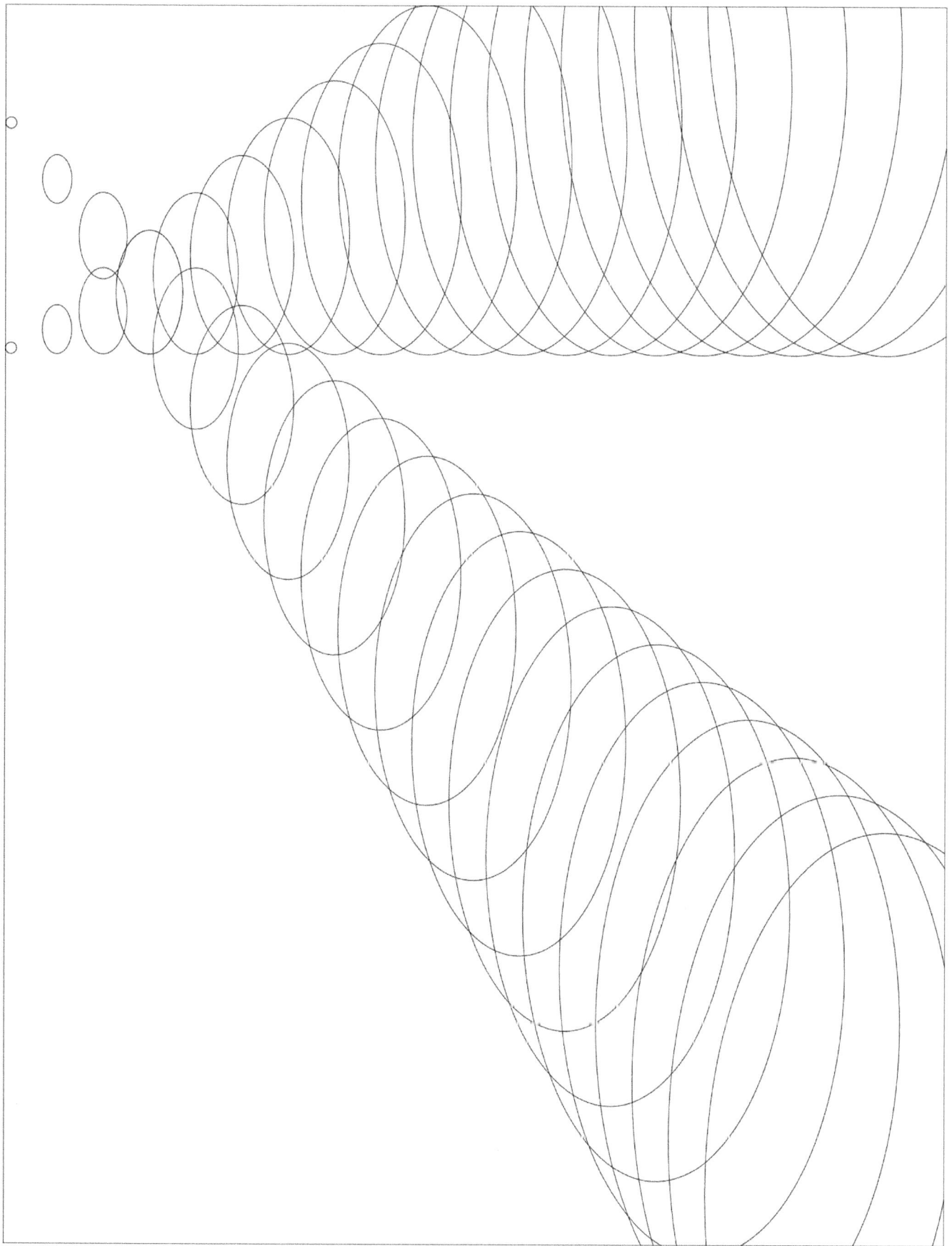

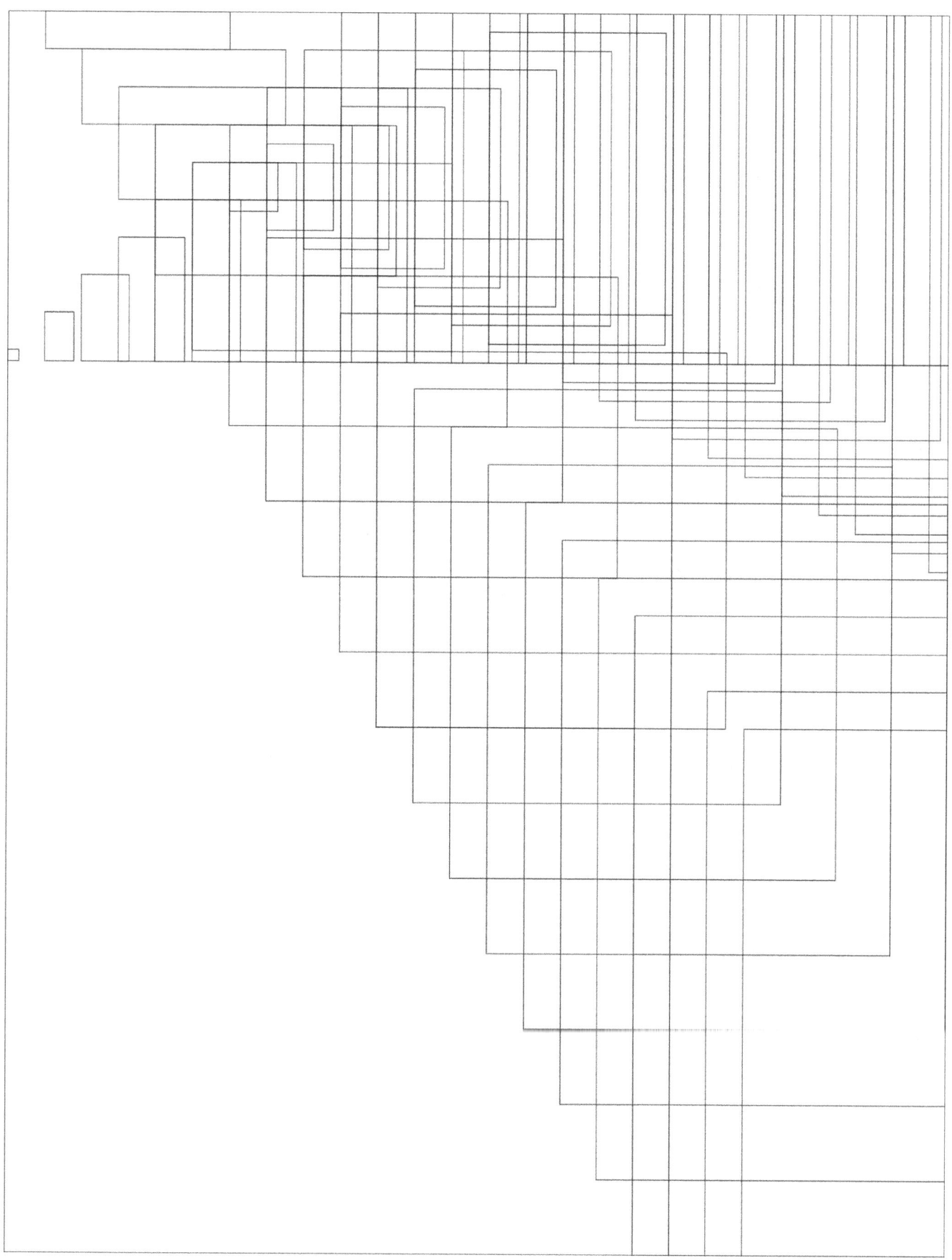

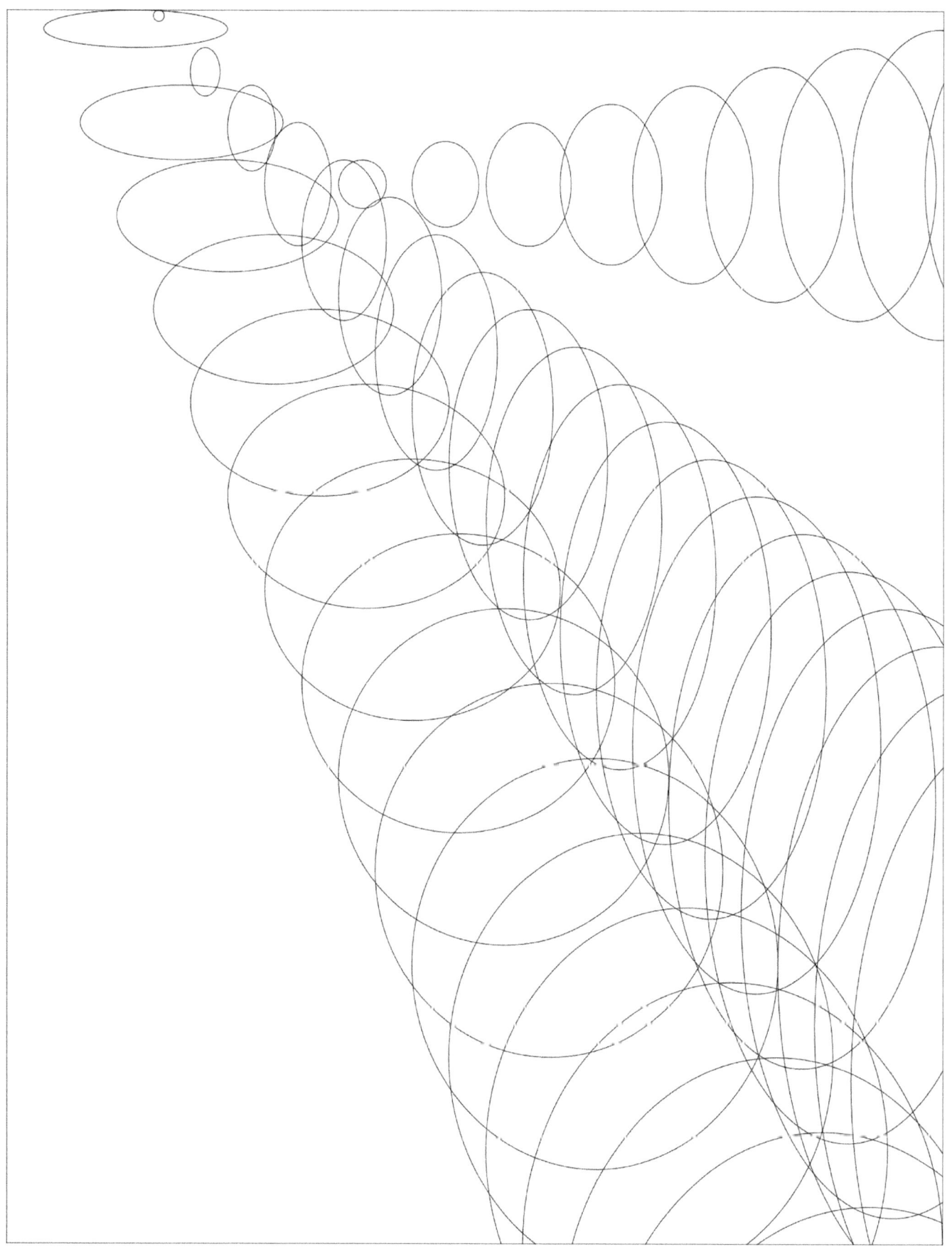

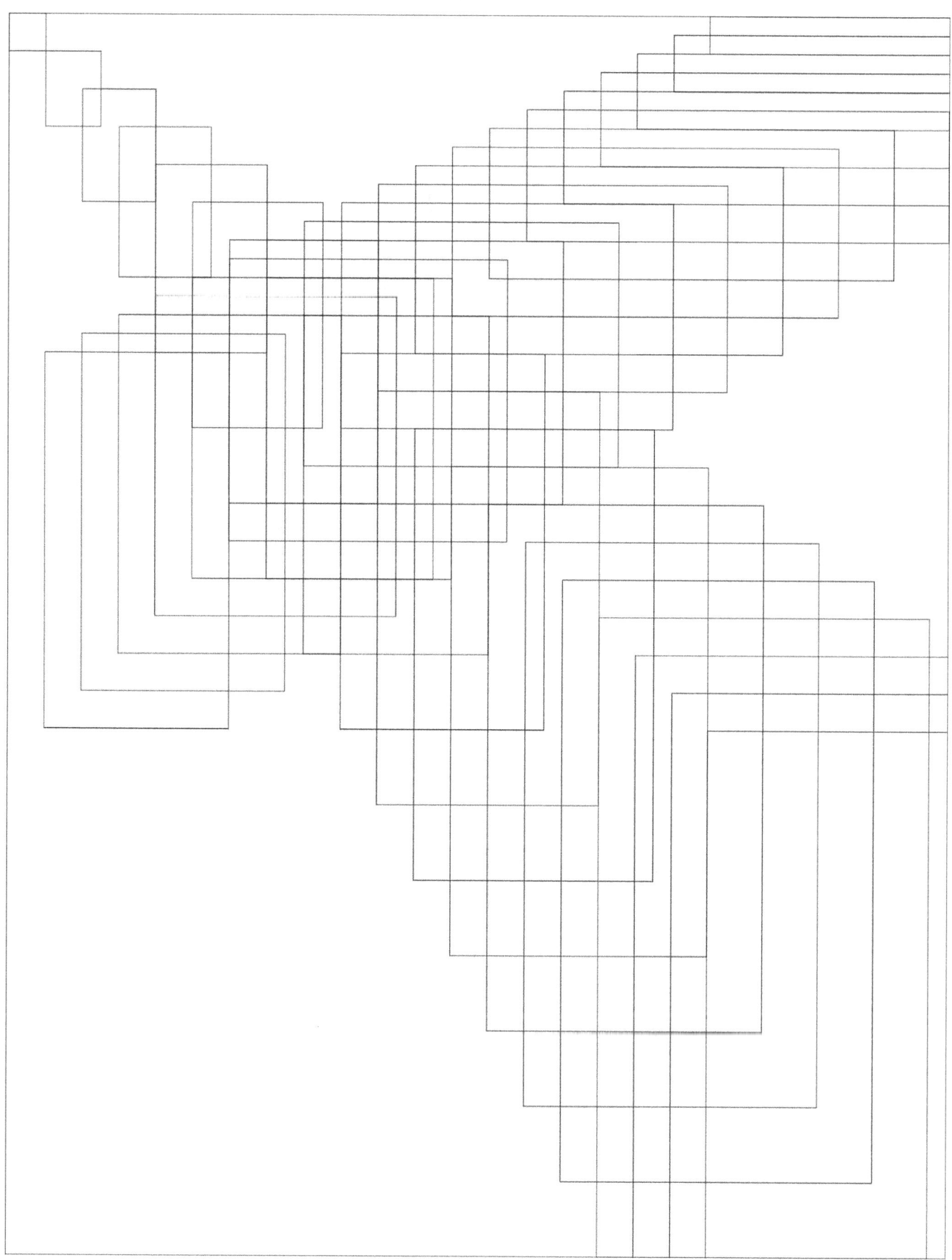

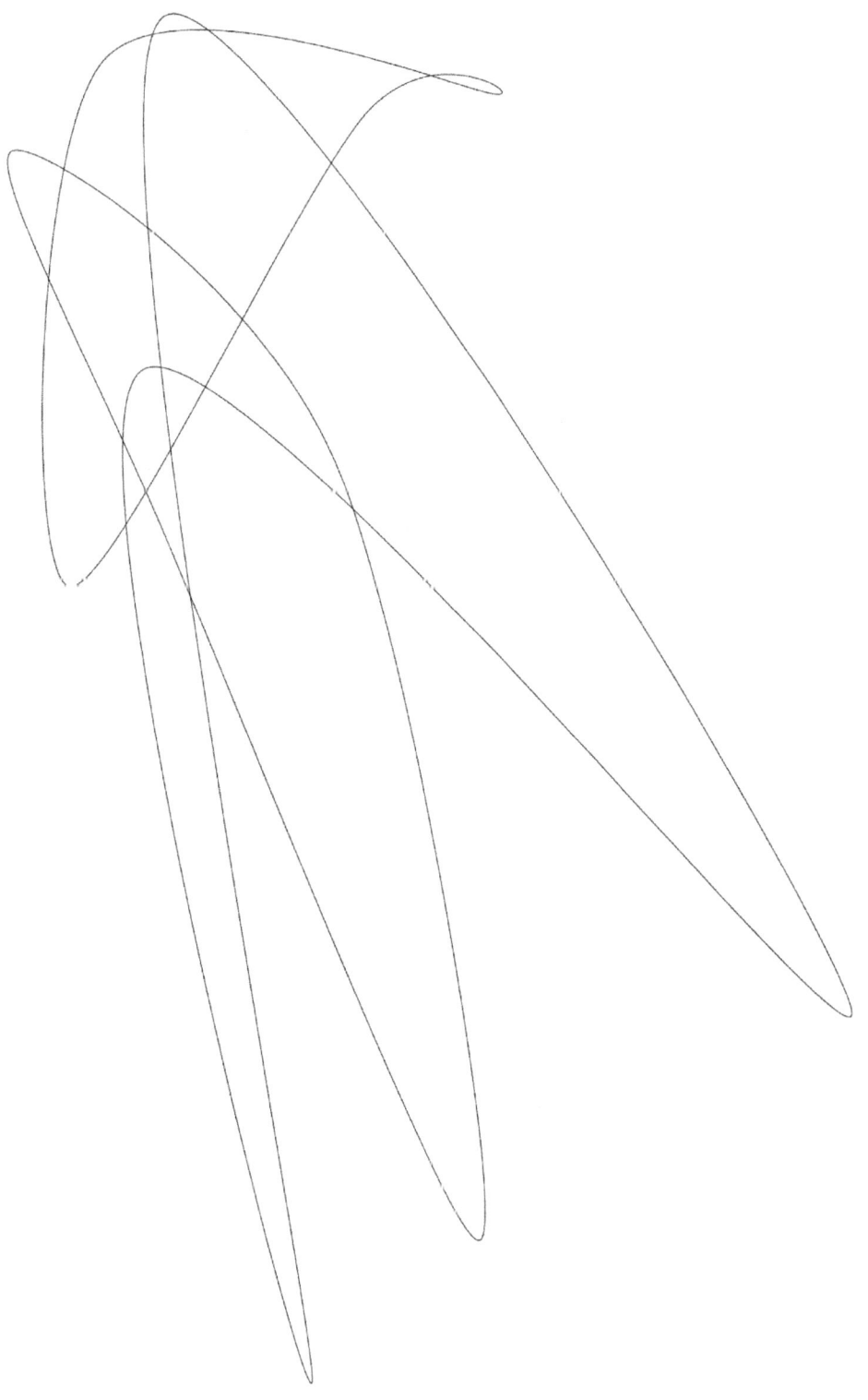

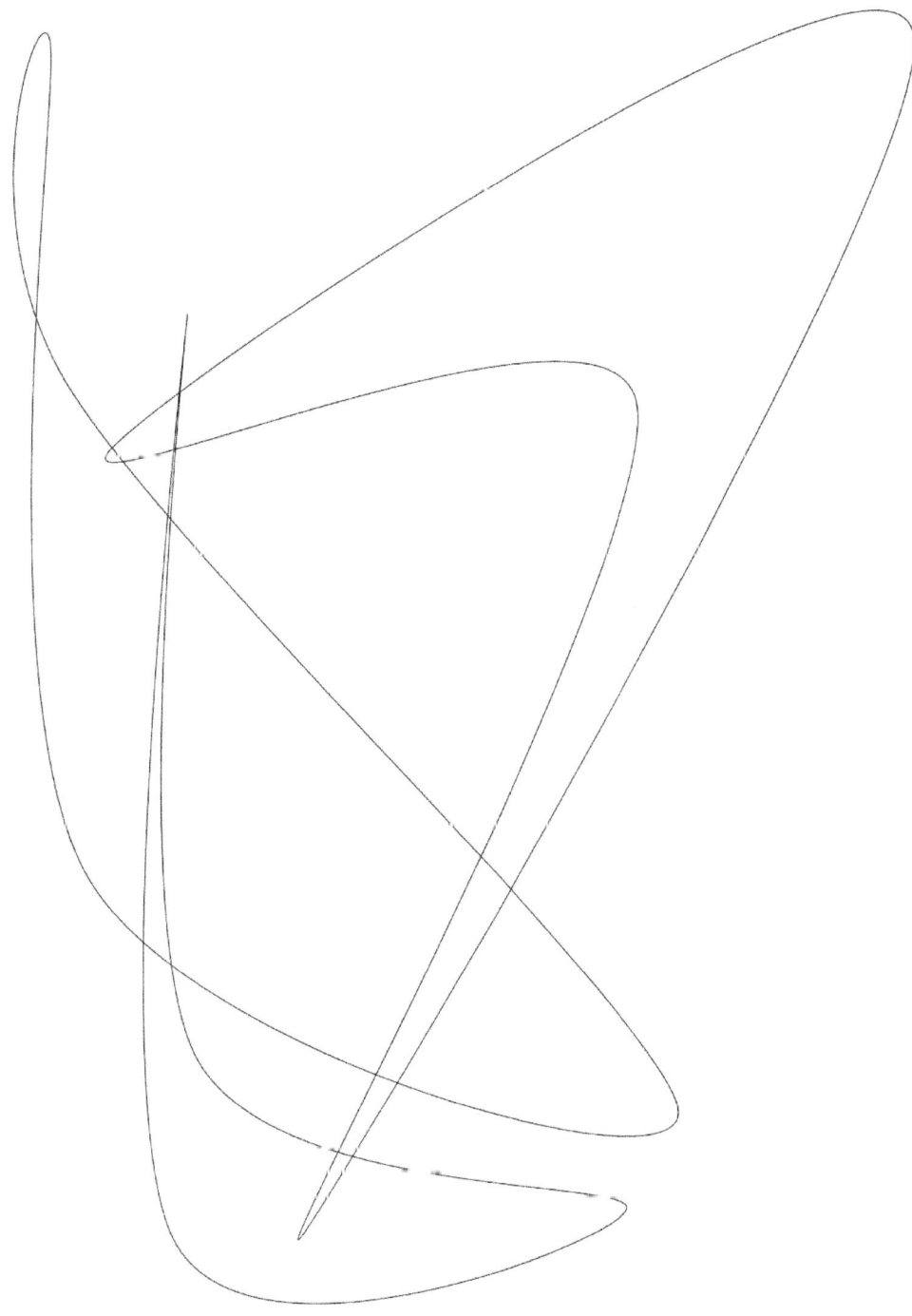

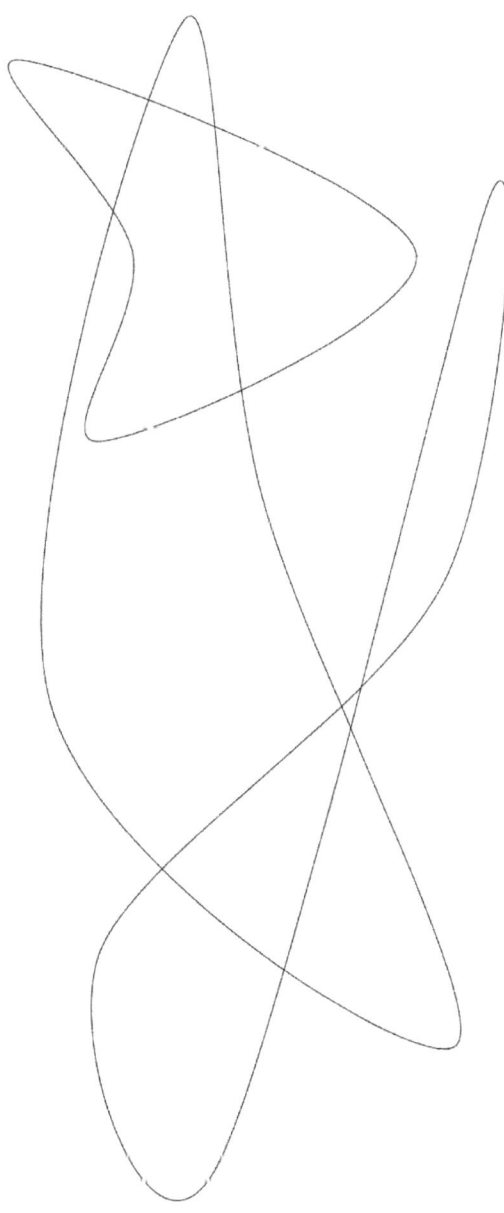

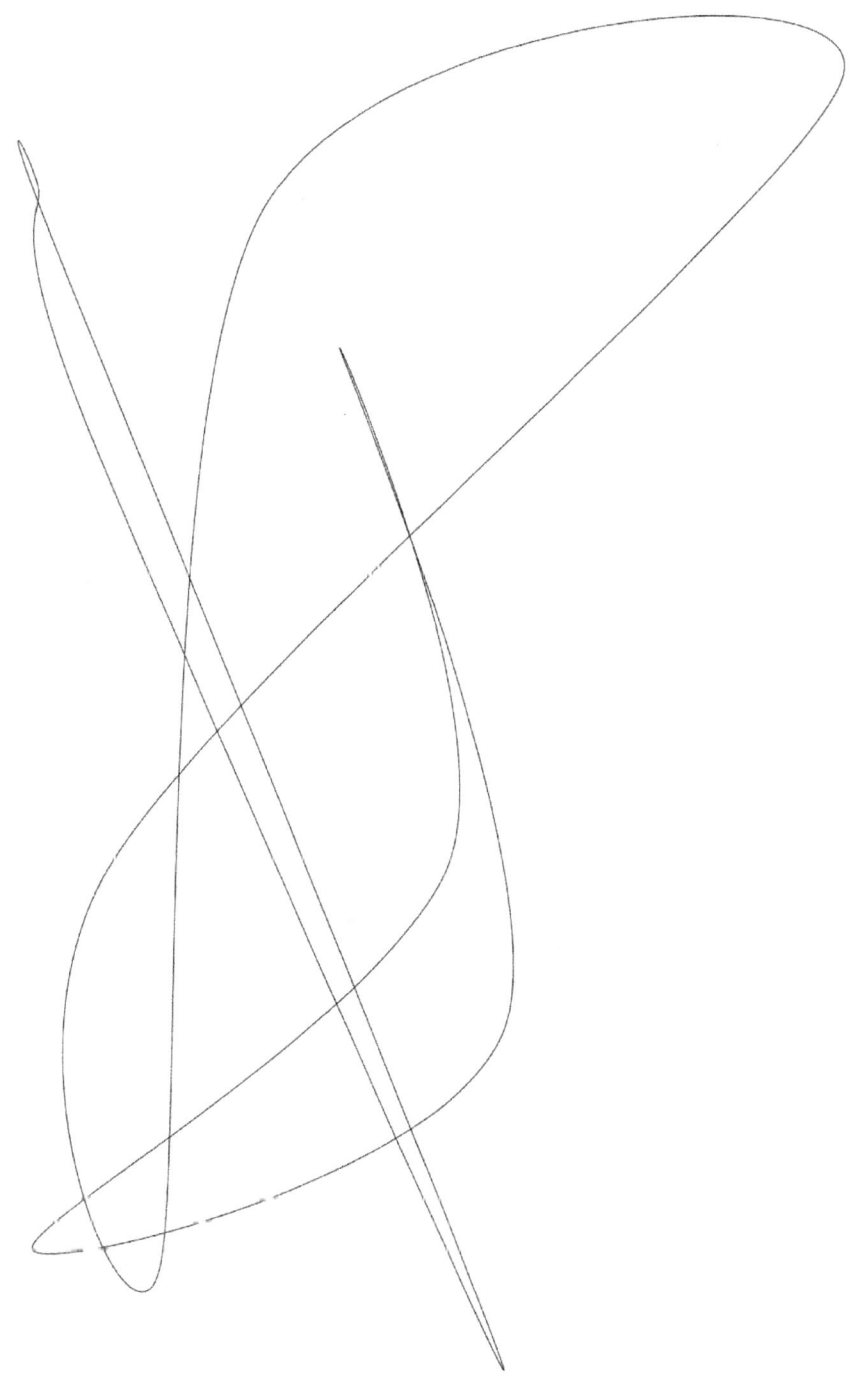

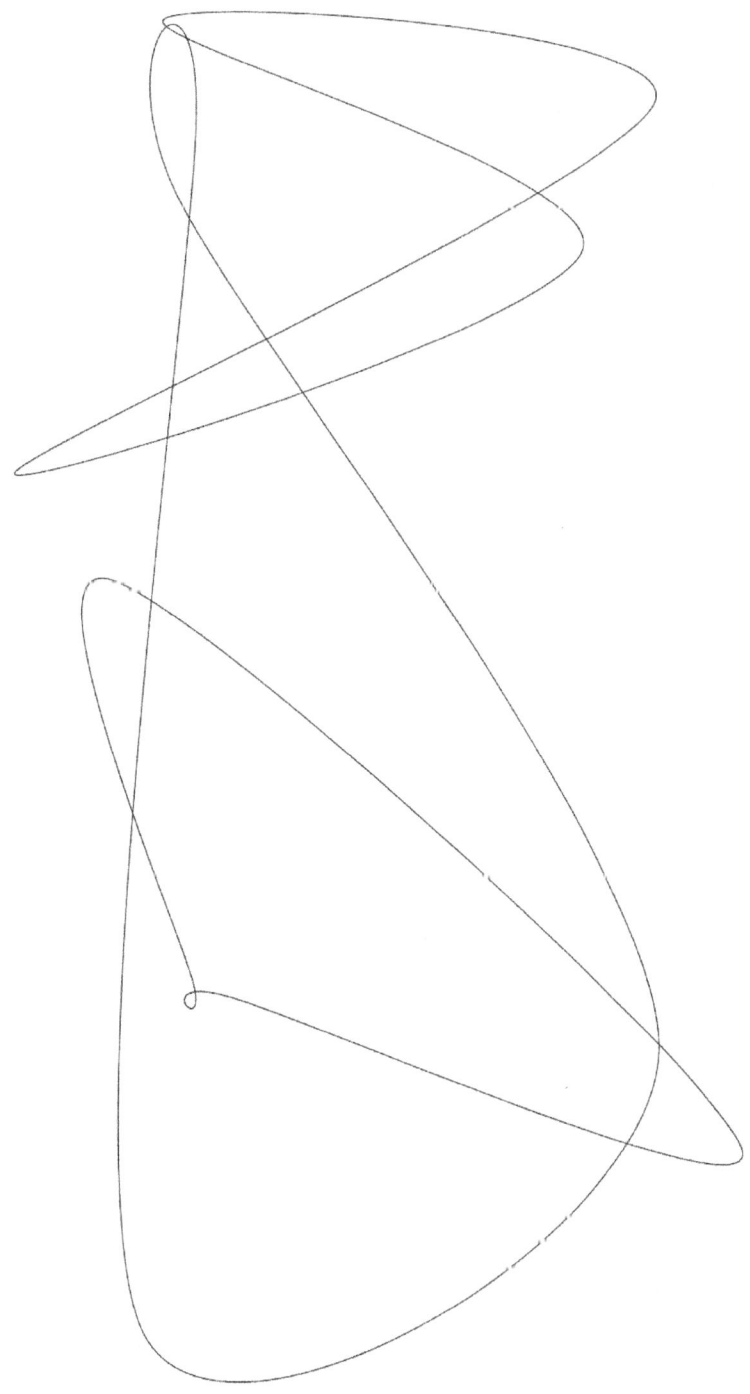

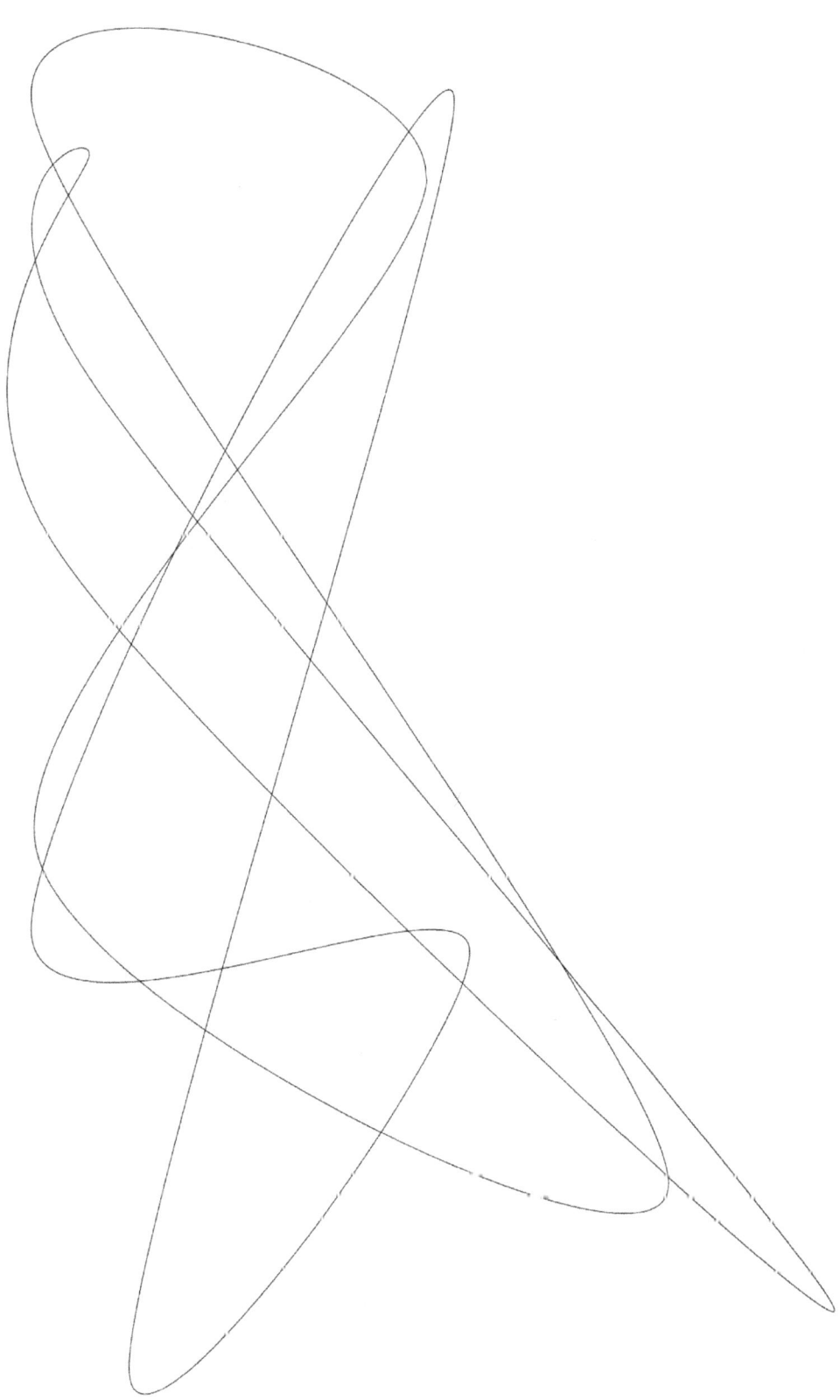

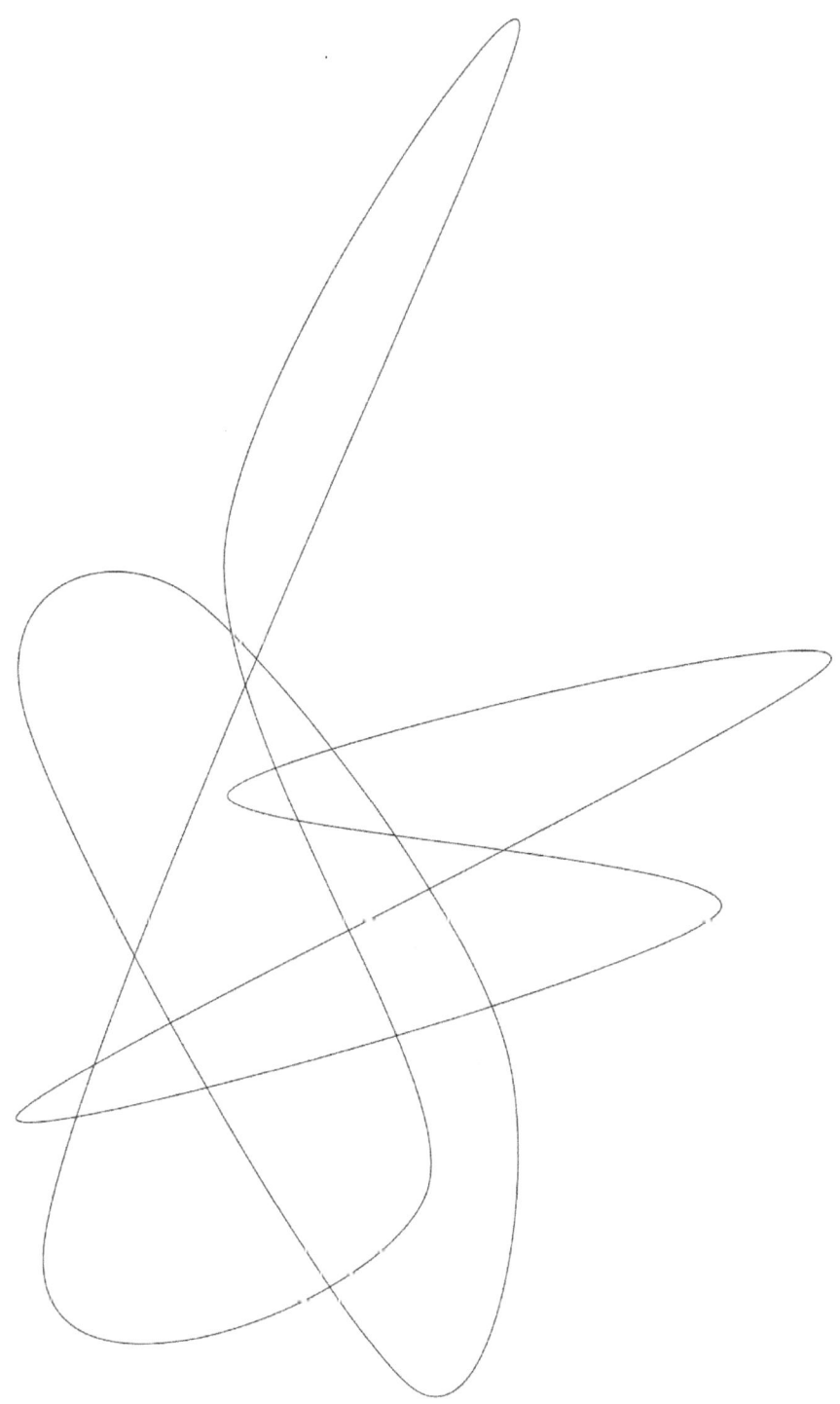

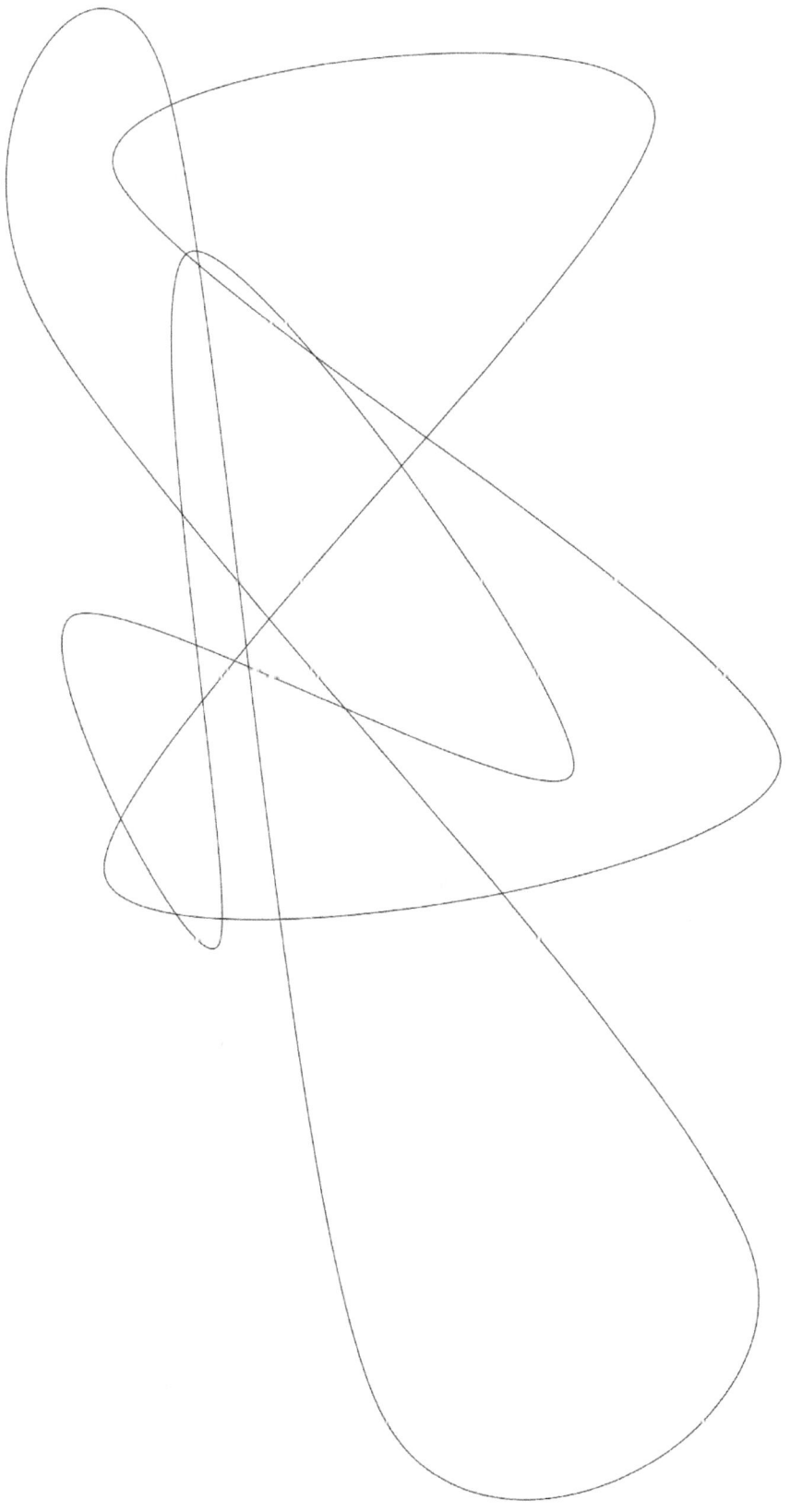

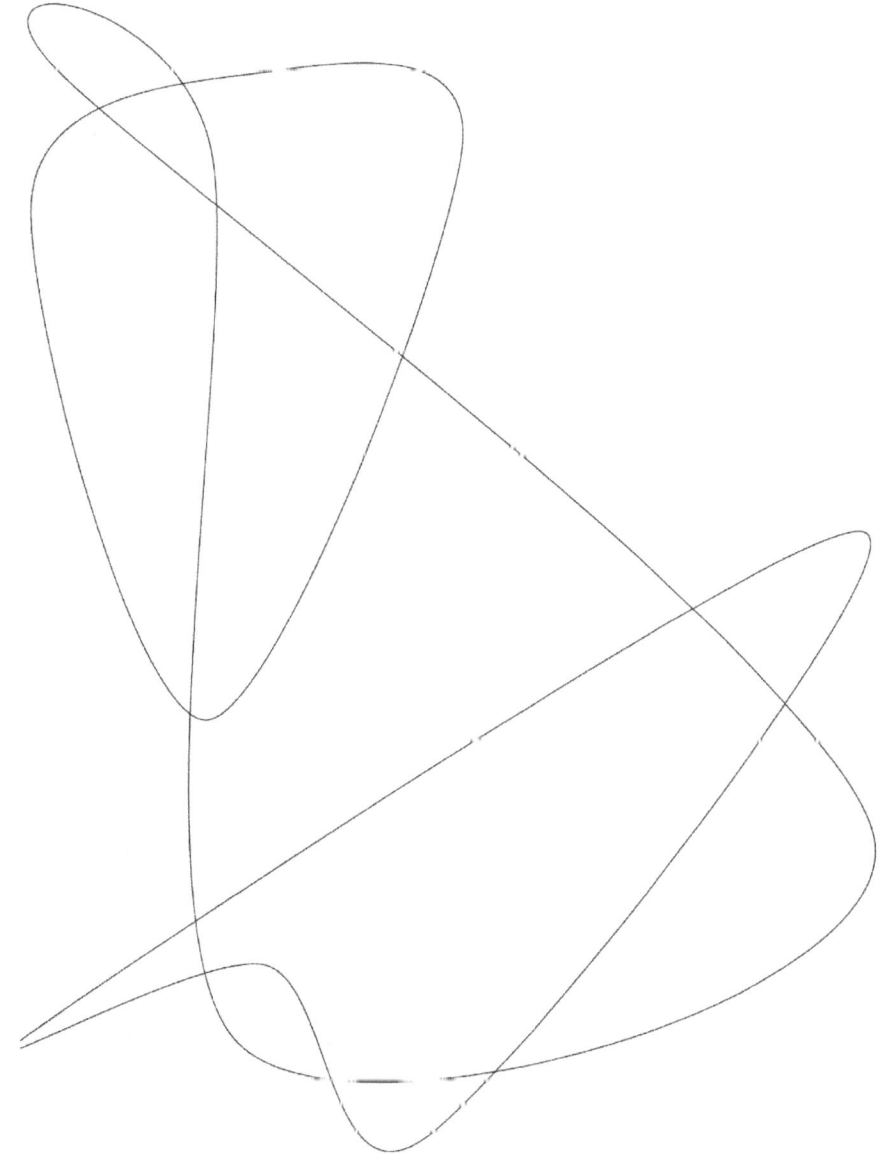

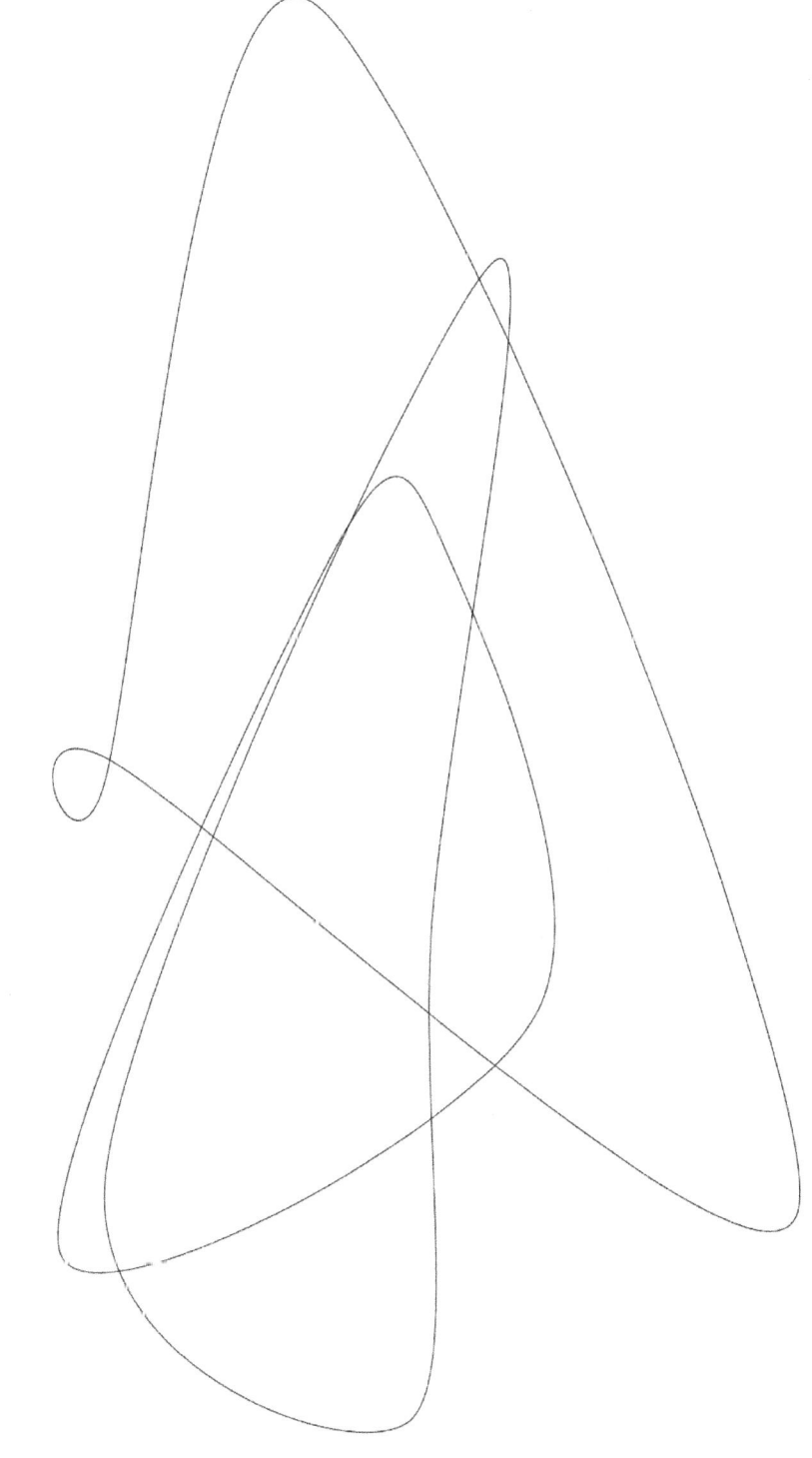

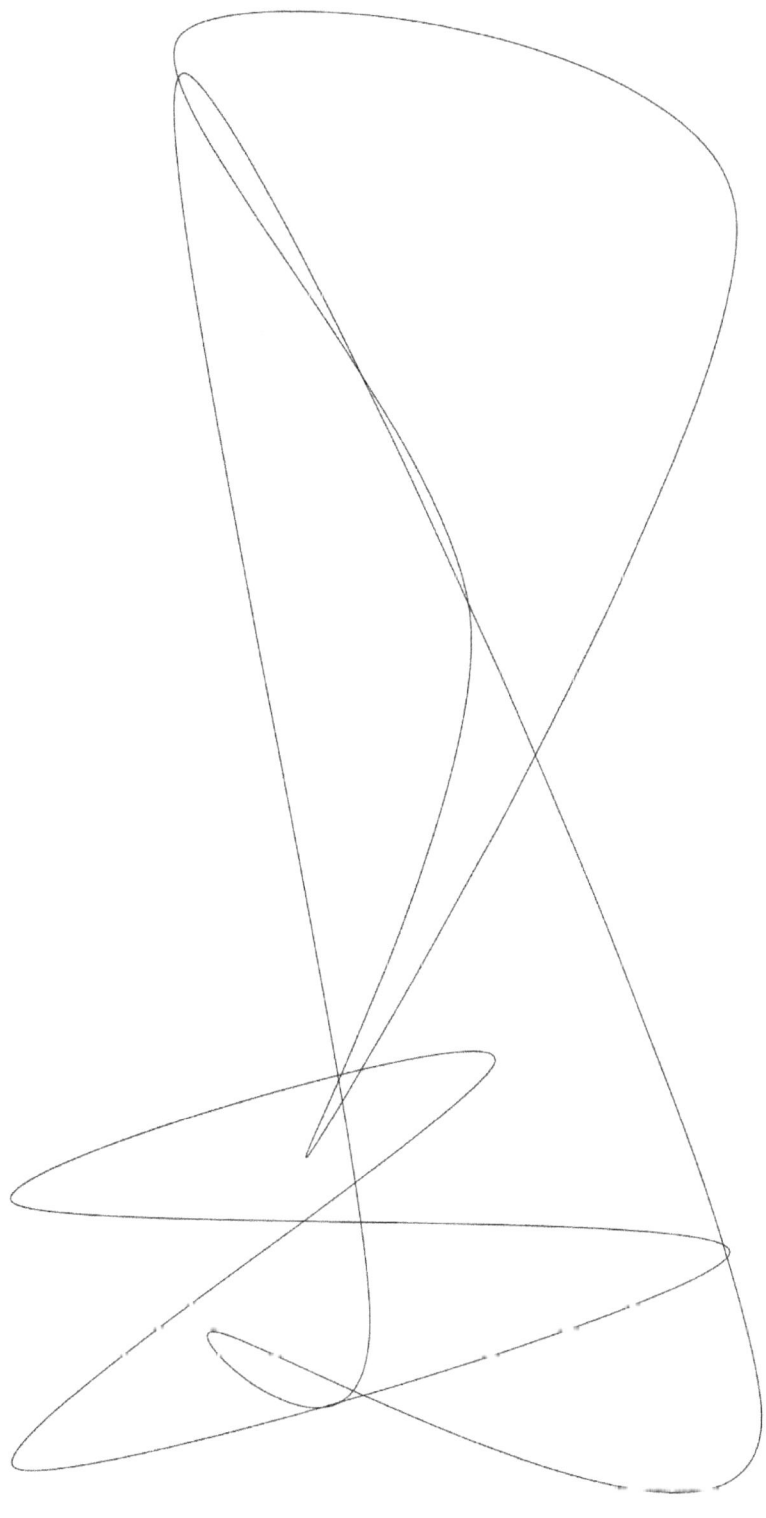

J. Mummey

J. Mummey

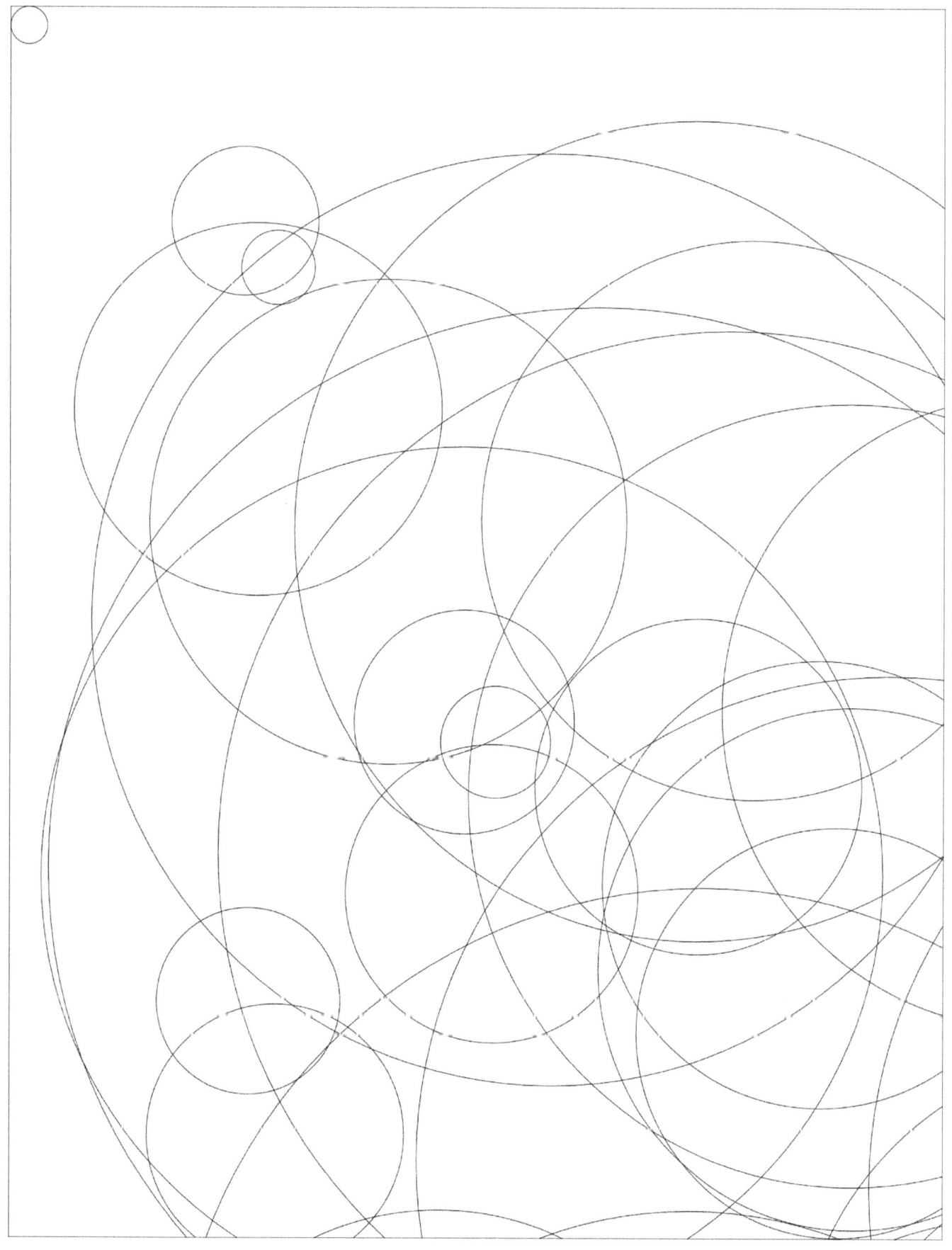

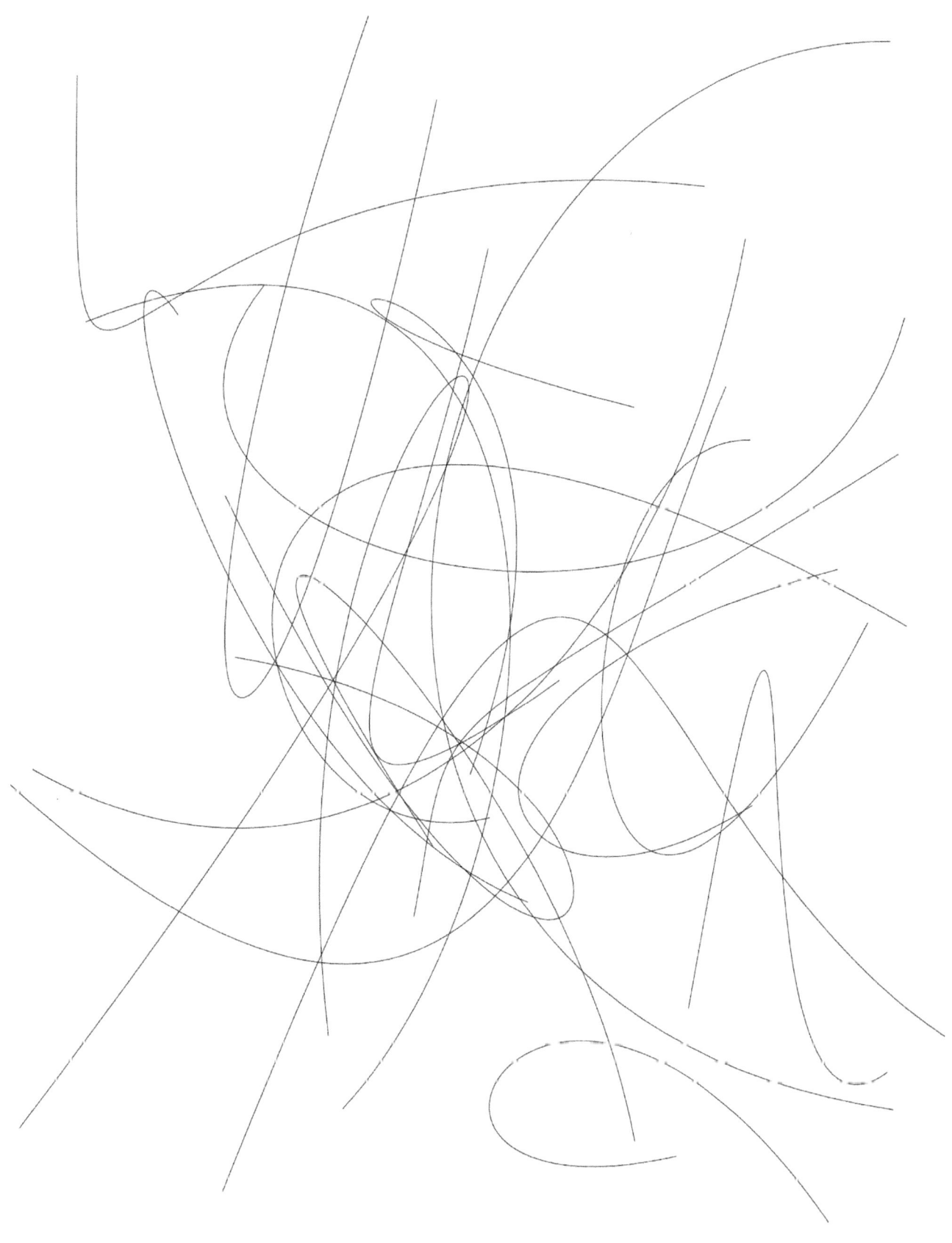

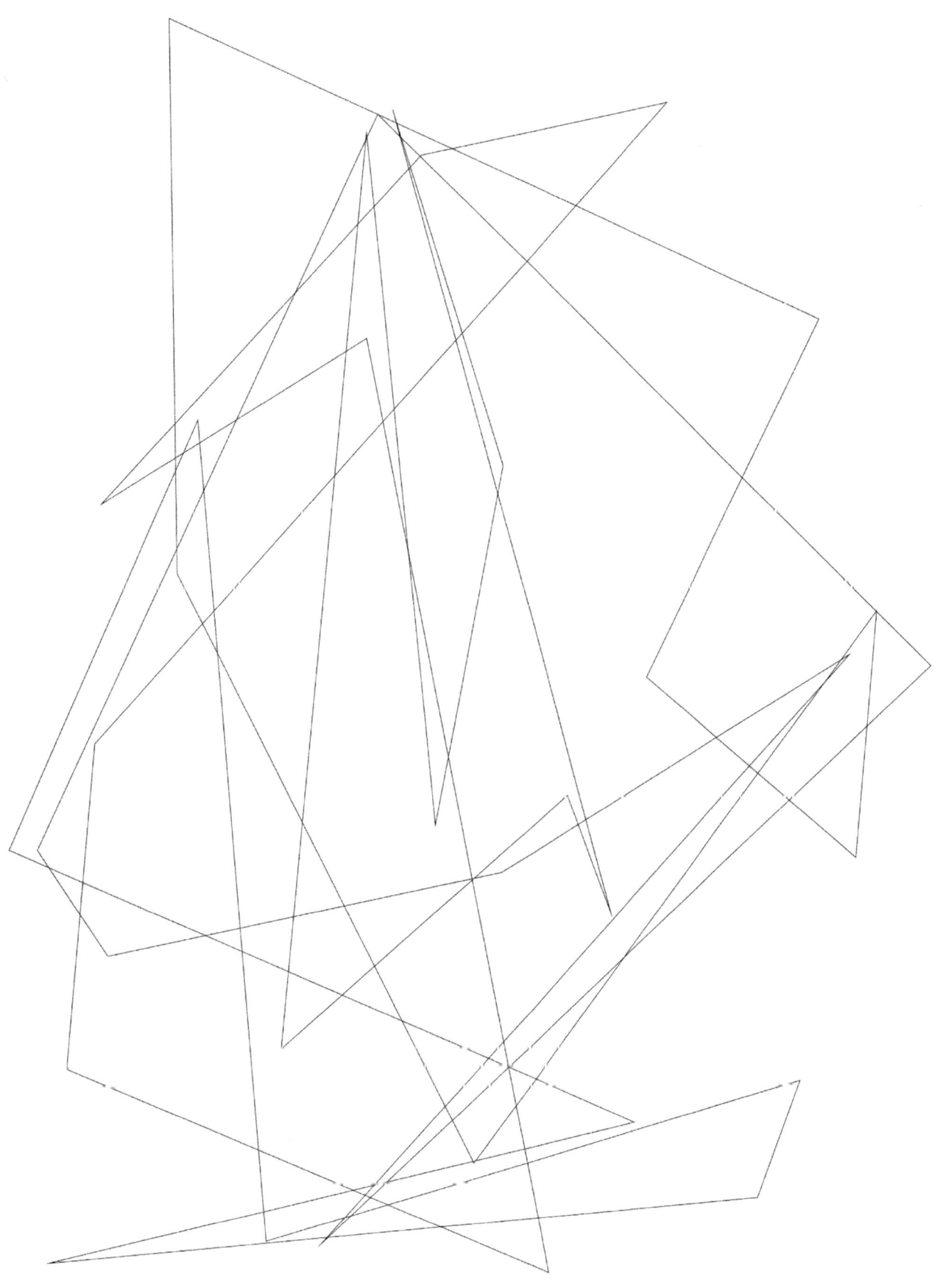

J. Mummey

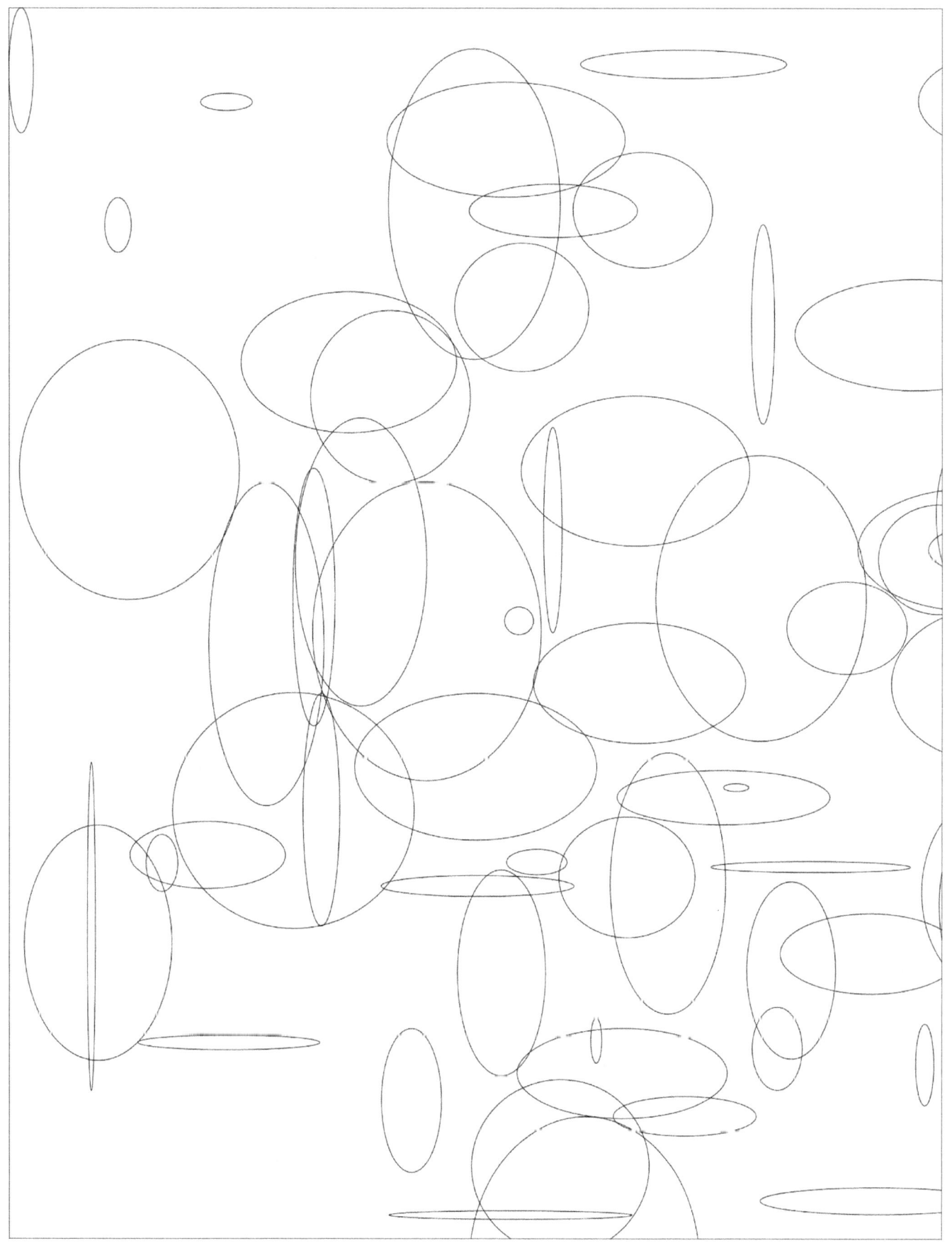

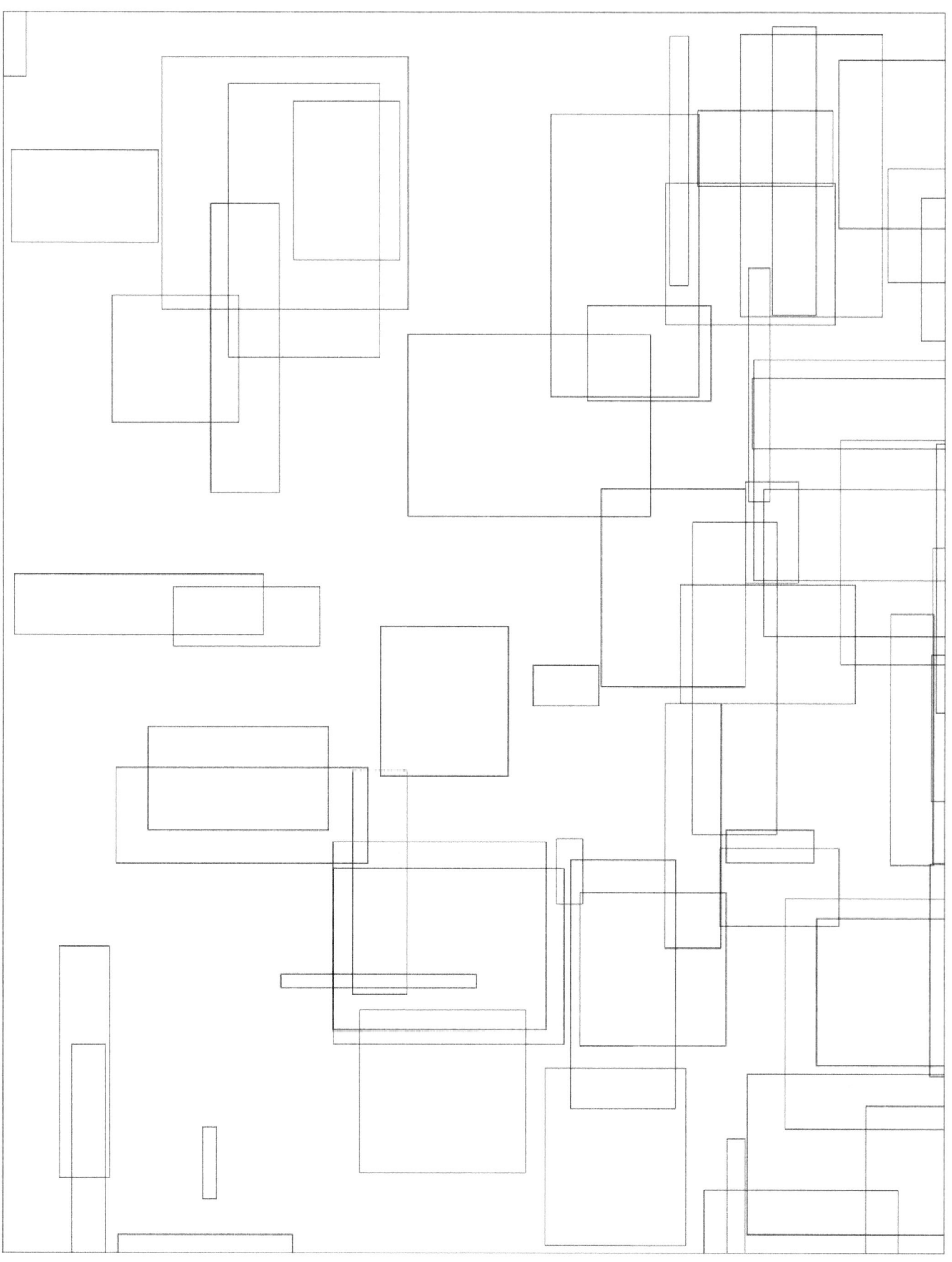

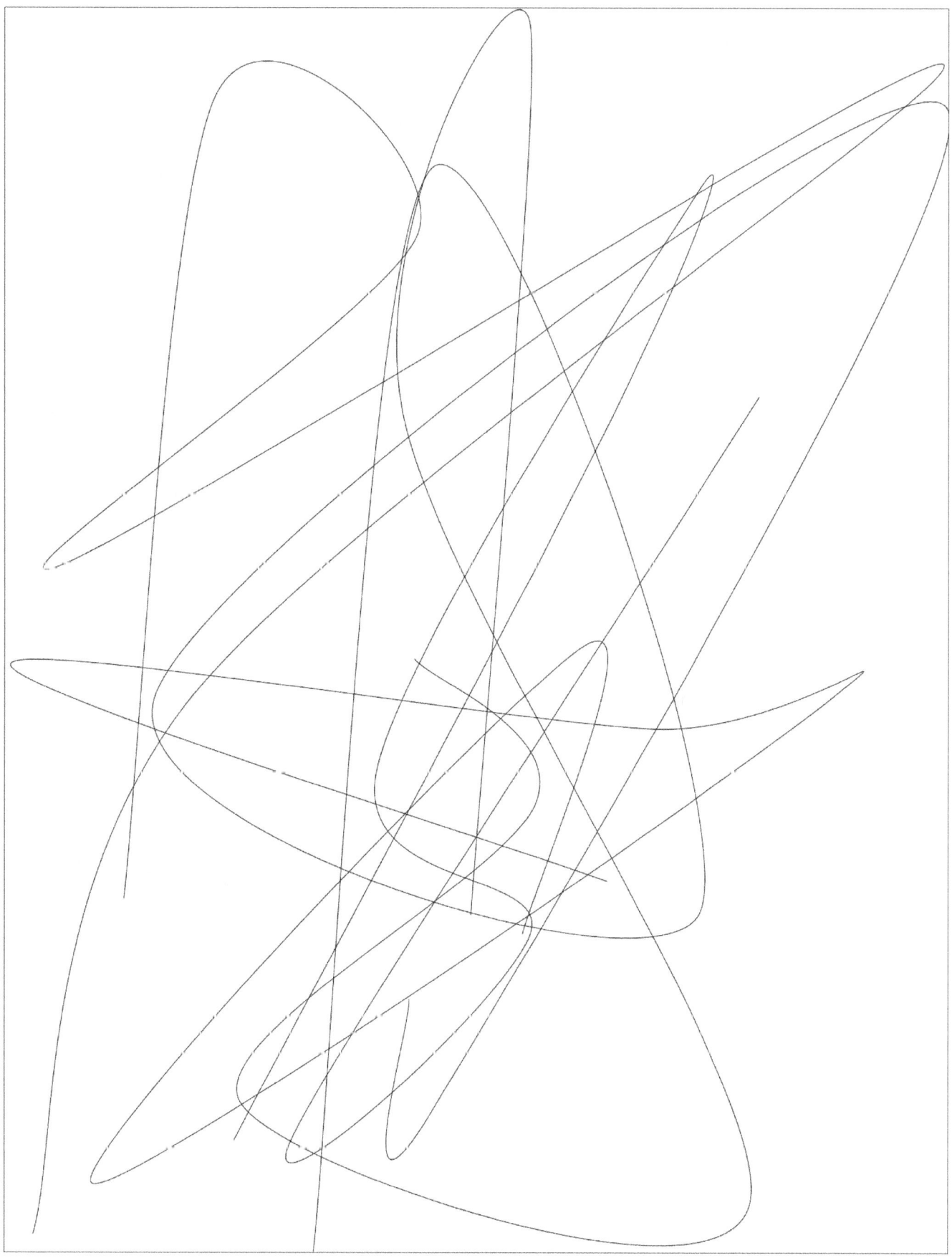

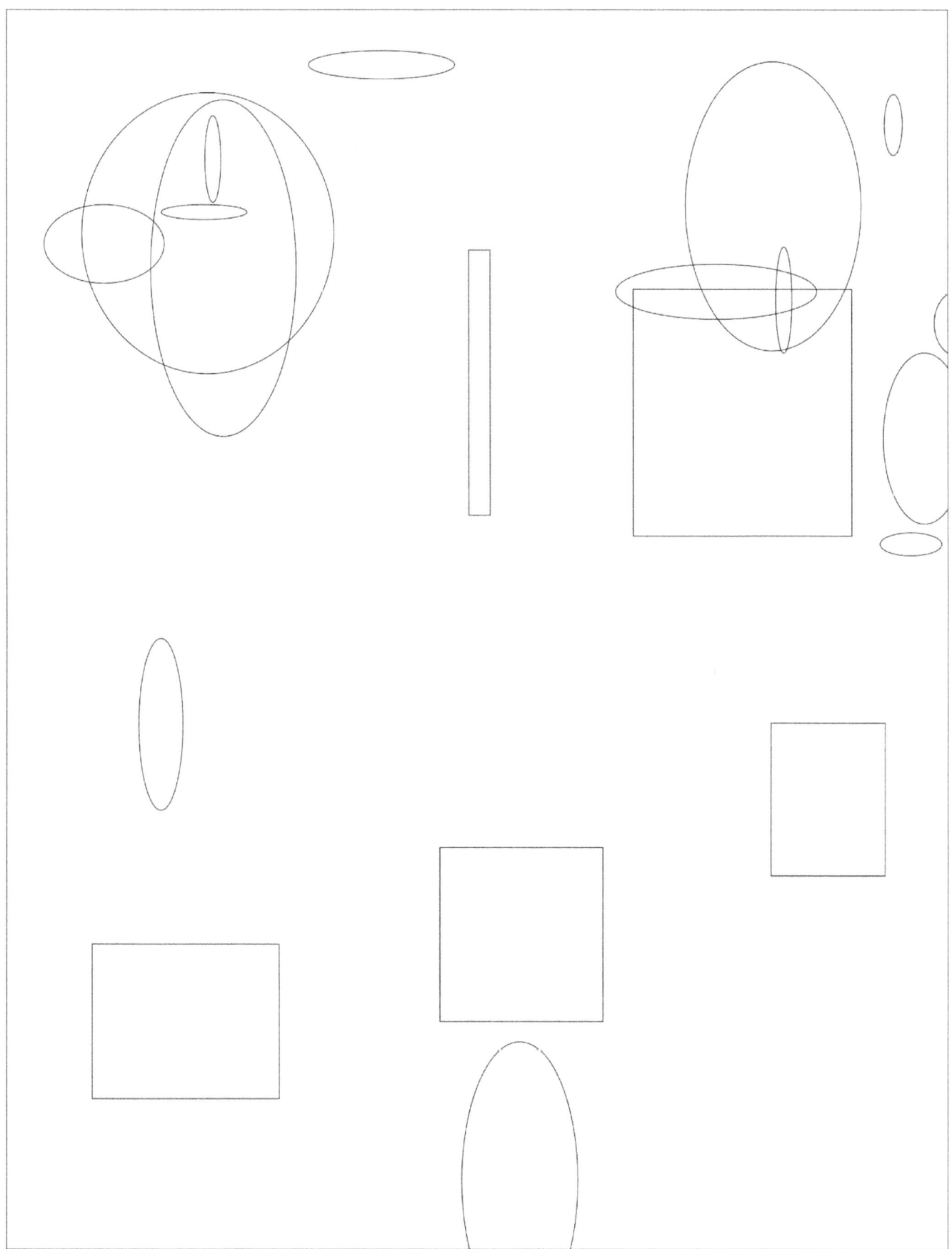

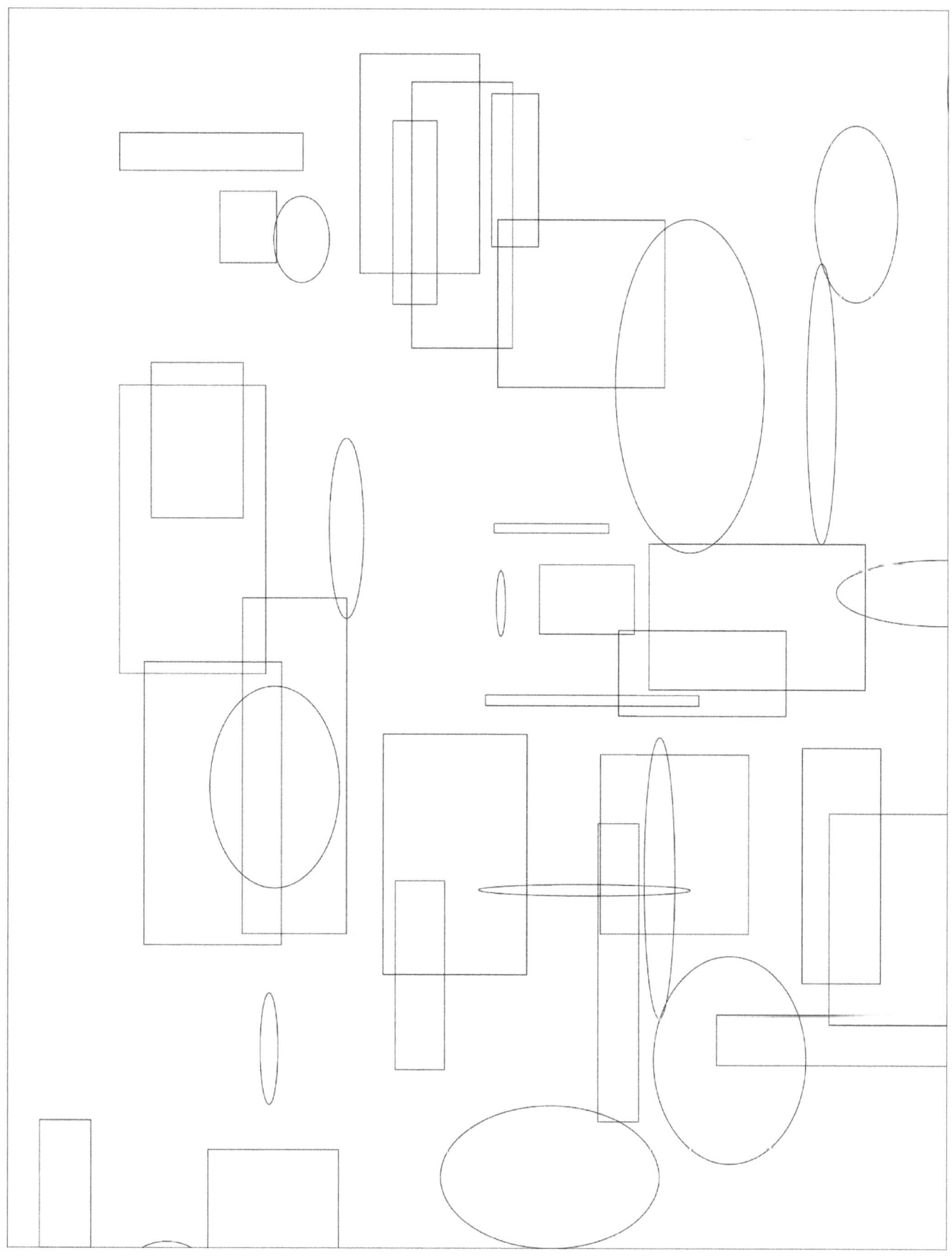

ABOUT THE AUTHOR

J. Mummey is a computer programmer, writer and terrible chess player living in Raleigh, North Carolina.

www.ingramcontent.com/pod-product-compliance
Lightning Source LLC
Chambersburg PA
CBHW081153180526
45170CB00006B/2066